NO MORE EXCUSES GET OUT AND GROW

RAISED-BED GARDENING EXPLAINED PLUS 5 SECRETS TO SUPERCHARGE ANY GARDEN

G. GREY

© Copyright 2023 - **All rights reserved.**

The content contained within this book may not be reproduced, duplicated or transmitted without direct written permission from the author or the publisher.

Under no circumstances will any blame or legal responsibility be held against the publisher, or author, for any damages, reparation, or monetary loss due to the information contained within this book, either directly or indirectly.

Legal Notice:

This book is copyright protected. It is only for personal use. You cannot amend, distribute, sell, use, quote or paraphrase any part, or the content within this book, without the consent of the author or publisher.

Disclaimer Notice:

Please note the information contained within this document is for educational and entertainment purposes only. All effort has been executed to present accurate, up to date, reliable, complete information. No warranties of any kind are declared or implied. Readers acknowledge that the author is not engaged in the rendering of legal, financial, medical or professional advice. The content within this book has been derived from various sources. Please consult a licensed professional before attempting any techniques outlined in this book.

By reading this document, the reader agrees that under no circumstances is the author responsible for any losses, direct or indirect, that are incurred as a result of the use of the information contained within this document, including, but not limited to, errors, omissions, or inaccuracies.

CONTENTS

Introduction   9

1. WHY RAISED BED GARDENING?   17
   What Are Raised Garden Beds?   18
   Benefits of Raised Garden Beds   20
   The Disadvantages of Raised Garden Beds   27
   Wrapping It Up   29

2. IMPORTANCE OF GOOD SOIL PLUS FIVE SECRETS TO SUPERCHARGE YOUR GARDEN   31
   What Is Healthy Soil?   32
   How to Build Raised Garden Beds With Healthy Soil   34
   Tips to Improve the Quality of Your Soil   39
   How to Overcome Deficiencies   42
   Five Secrets to Supercharge Your Garden   46

3. PLANNING YOUR GARDEN   53
   Planning Tips   54
   Bed Box Tips   59
   Planting Tips   62
   A Couple of General Tips   66

4. IDEAS FOR RAISED BEDS PLUS FIVE LOW-COST BEDS   69
   Wood Boards   70
   Wooden Tiered Beds   71
   Wood Frames Coupled with Steel Roofing   72
   Concrete Blocks   73
   Steel Beds   75

Hardie-Plank Siding Boards	76
Concrete Paver Beds	77
Composite Deck Beds	77
Gabion Beds	78
Split Log Beds	79
DIY Log Bed	81
The Most Affordable Alternatives	82

5. PLANTING AND COMPANION PLANTS — 93
- Looking Back on Companion Planting — 95
- Benefits of Companion Gardening — 96
- Companion Planting Relationships — 98
- Different Ways to Companion Plant — 107
- Incompatible Plants — 108

6. MULCHING AND WATERING — 113
- What Is Mulch? — 114
- When to Mulch? — 120
- Why Should You Mulch? — 120
- A Few Mulching Tips — 123
- Watering — 124
- Alternative Watering Solutions — 127

7. FENCING/PLANTING FLOWERS TO KEEP PESTS AWAY — 135
- Natural Ways to Address Garden Pests — 136
- Steps You Can Take When Spotting Pests — 145
- The Most Common Garden Pests — 149
- The Importance of Fencing — 151

8. PLANT PROFILES/PLANT HARDINESS CHARTS — 157
- Hardiness Zones Explained — 158
- The Best Veggies to Grow in Your Garden — 163

Conclusion	179
Author Bio	185
Acknowledgments	187
Bibliography	191

*This book is dedicated to GOD.
The original gardener and creator of The Garden of Eden.
"We give thanks to You, God, we give thanks! For Your wondrous works declare that Your name is near."
-Psalm 75:1*

INTRODUCTION

We might think that we are nurturing our garden, but in fact, it is our garden that is nurturing us.

— UNKNOWN

What if I told you that there is one activity that is known for reducing stress while also helping you burn calories, improve your immune system, and does wonders to create balance in your life. That it is linked to reducing your chances of getting a stroke and improves your sensory systems, your sense of creativity, and even your gut health. It is an activity in which each member of your family can partake, and while doing so, you will be strengthening your bonds. It helps to give older family members a sense of purpose and teaches the younger generation a sense of responsibility. The best part of all is that you can eat the fruits of your labor. Would you be interested in getting to know all there is about this life-changing activity?

While the expression of disbelief I have seen when I make this statement is surely something I will always remember, it is nothing compared to the expressions I see when I reveal what this secret activity is...*gardening*.

Gardening is an age-old tradition upheld in many cultures, not only for food production but also for mental stimulation and as a way to create spaces of emotional tranquility. I have been fortunate to travel as my career in the military took me to many places across the globe. My mother was an avid gardener with the magical ability to grow anything she planted and she passed her love to nurture life out of the soil on to me.

Hence, I have always been interested in and explored gardens and gardening practices whenever I found myself in a new country. It is how I managed to learn gardening practices from around the world, practices that influenced and improved my own gardening skills and gave me access to a diversity of techniques. Not only did I adopt these techniques in my own garden, but I also adjusted them to suit the specific climate conditions where I am currently based in the wilds of British Columbia, Canada. Here, most of my gardening activities take place in a 65 x 15 ft greenhouse; a great space that provides us with fresh produce all year round.

Throughout the years I have had many friends and family members—and at times complete strangers—reach out to learn more about gardening; an activity that has enjoyed an increasing interest over the past couple of years. We are experiencing an emerging awareness of how our food is produced and the number of people keen on growing produce in their own back gardens is increasing. This is a notion that I support wholeheartedly as there are no healthier food options than the vegetables you have grown yourself, from the soil you have cared for all year round.

Yet, this can be a challenging quest if you have limited knowledge of gardening or how to care for the space so that it can produce optimally. While some of the questions I get are related to bringing out the best in existing gardens, there is also a growing interest from those who have never dipped their fingers in the soil before and therefore have no idea where to start.

Gardening does not have to be an expensive venture, but if you proceed blindly, it might mean that you will start accruing unnecessary expenses. A lack of knowledge and skills could also lead to persistent failure which can be disheartening. If you identify with the latter, then I am excited for you as every tip and trick, word of gardening advice, and guideline I am sharing will prevent you from experiencing yet another failure.

You have already proven your persistence by picking up this book and now I can help you to reap the fruits of your labor—literally and figuratively.

That said, I am as excited about the newbie gardener. By putting every skill I share into practice, you will soon enjoy the outcome you have been hoping for—a flourishing garden with crops you can harvest and food you can serve for the enjoyment—and admiration—of your friends and family.

We start this venture at the very beginning and I will answer the questions of what a raised bed garden is, what the benefits linked to this type of gardening are, and why I prefer this gardening technique. Next, we explore soil and how to care for it. Soil may appear dead, but it is very much alive and the better you care for your soil, the greater your results will be. Failing to plan is planning to fail, right? So, we have to include garden planning to ensure that your design is practical and effective. I have mentioned before that gardening does not have to be an expensive venture, especially not if you know what you are doing. Therefore, I share all you need to know about low-cost beds.

Then, you should be ready to plant. Did you know that some plants do much better when they are surrounded by their own kind while other plants grow best when in the company of specific other species? In the world of gardening, we refer to the latter as companion planting. While you may have already placed a lot of emphasis on preparing the soil before you plant, you also have to sustain the quality of the soil throughout the year. This is where mulching and watering play a crucial role in your success.

Gardens resemble life and as they are part of nature, they will surely attract all kinds of life, including some unwanted visitors. Pests can create devastation in a small amount of time, so I will share all the knowledge you need to protect your garden from them.

While vegetable gardening brings food to the table, flowers feed the soul, so perhaps you are leaning more towards growing a garden for these natural beauties. And to be honest, a book on gardening would just not be complete without exploring flower gardening too.

When it comes to gardening, there are many variables you have control over, but also those which you have no control over at all. Hardiness zones fall into the latter category. Exploring these zones and how you can optimize the conditions of the zone you are located in is a perfect way to bring our discussion on gardening to an end.

So, what is the vision you have for your garden? What do you want to achieve from this venture and which benefits of gardening are the ones you look forward to most?

Just imagine pondering these questions while sitting in your beautiful garden we are about to create. Does this image not inspire you to jump right into it?

Now, no more excuses, get out and grow.

1

WHY RAISED BED GARDENING?

To plant a garden is to believe in tomorrow.

— UNKNOWN

The more you get involved in gardening, the more you will discover the various ways to produce practical and attractive crops. As an avid gardener who has been fortunate enough to see how gardeners across the globe produce crops in a variety of ways, I have been able to try several different ways of gardening. However, I always find myself returning to raised garden beds. I do this not only because it is a way of gardening that I have grown up with, and maybe even feel a bit sentimental about, but because there are so many benefits to using raised garden beds. But before I expand on the benefits you will enjoy from this type of gardening, I want to explain what it is exactly.

WHAT ARE RAISED GARDEN BEDS?

Raised garden beds are basically when you build your beds on top of the surface of the existing soil rather than having them on the same level as the soil. Examples are flower or vegetable boxes placed on the surface and filled with planting soil. These boxes can be built from wood, concrete, stone, or as we will discover later on, a range of other practical materials and can add aesthetic appeal to your garden. Some of these options are more expensive to build, but we will also look at a couple of far more affordable raised bed options.

These boxes can be placed on covered surfaces, for example on a paved area, or directly onto the surface of the soil without having a protective layer between the soil in the box and the soil surface.

It is a way of planting that dates back to medieval times when these boxes were often used as property borders. Much later on, gardeners of the Parisian market would gather manure from the horses used for transport to build up their garden beds. As often happens with ancient practices, they become outdated only to be rediscovered years, or centuries later. So, in the 1970s raised bed gardening became popular again. The gardens of this era contained raised beds as clear property markers to prevent others from accidentally walking through their crops. As you can only imagine, after heavy rains, gardeners would have to do some serious repairs as the soil from these beds would wash away into the pathways. This is why the trend changed to include physical constraints like wood or stone, to ensure the heaped soil stays intact. Since then, this type of gardening has grown in popularity to grow flowers and vegetables.

BENEFITS OF RAISED GARDEN BEDS

So, why do I continue to return to this kind of planting? I am confident that after looking at the reasons below, you will see that raised garden beds make gardening so much easier.

Better Results With Less Effort

Say you have identified a spot in your backyard that you would like to use for a vegetable garden. Even though it might not be a large area, once you start working on it, you become painfully aware of how many weeds you need to take out and the amount of compost you need to work into the area to get healthy soil. This kind of gardening can quickly require a high level of investment of time and money and not yield the crops you expected. On the contrary, if you use a raised garden bed, you will have much greater control over the quality of the soil and it will require a smaller investment of your time and money, bringing you great returns in the form of produce.

Plenty of Root Space

When you construct your beds or decide what kind of containers you are going to use, you first have to consider what you are going to plant in them. Certain types of vegetables do not require much soil as their root systems are not as developed. However, if you build the beds too shallow, you will limit yourself to what you can plant in them. The idea is to never opt for planter boxes less than one foot deep but ideally, you should get raised beds that are between 18-24 inches high.

Better Quality Soil

When you are preparing that piece of soil in your back yard, you have limited control over what type of soil you can work with as it is a case of working with what you have. When you create raised beds instead, you have absolute freedom and control over the quality of soil you will be filling them up with. Having this control enables you to choose soil that is light and airy while still rich in minerals and nutrients, giving you exceptional results.

Raised beds also allow you to have different types of soil in every box as you may want to grow different kinds of plants and vegetables. Some vegetables do well in more sandy soil while others prefer more compacted soil to ensure great root systems, some plants prefer more water while others do better with less. When you have raised beds, you can create the perfect environment regardless of the needs of your plants.

Make Weeding Easy

For many gardeners, weeding remains the worst part of gardening. It can seem as if no plant ever grows as fast as weeds do. One day your beds are neat and free from weeds and the next day, the weeds may be standing two inches high already, towering above your seedlings. When you have raised beds, weeding becomes an easy task as the soil is much looser and the weeds pull out with minimal effort. As these beds are raised a bit off the ground, it is also easy to get to as there are no hard-to-reach places in the boxes.

The seeds that come from weeds are also far less likely to get into the soil of your raised beds. When the wind is blowing seeds around, it is mostly just above the surface of the ground, but as raised garden beds are higher than this surface, the weeds seeds are far less likely to end up growing in them. Particularly effective if you opted for waist high beds for reducing back strain.

Make Planting and Harvesting Easy

This point is closely linked to the previous one even though planting and harvesting are much more fun to do than weeding. When you harvest your crops from a vegetable garden, you will probably get dirty, find it hard to reach some of the crops you want to take home, and you may even damage some plants as you have to get in between them when gardening. When it comes to raised gardens, these beds consist of a much smaller area so every inch of your garden is easy to reach. You will not get as dirty and there will be no damage to nearby plants afterward.

Easy to Plan

Later on, we will discuss planning your garden in greater depth, but for now, I want to mention that there is a bit of planning necessary if you want to enjoy a constant flow of fresh vegetables from your garden. Sure it is easy to plan a garden if you are an experienced gardener, but if you are not, it can be hard to plan it well. Consider how much planning needs to go into keeping track of a large patch of soil, compared to raised garden beds that are smaller and symmetrically placed next to each other. These beds make it easy to plant rows and rotate what you plant in them.

Wonderful Versatility

Some types of gardens are restricted to a certain type of soil or can only flourish in certain hardiness zones. This is, for the most part, not the case when it comes to raised garden beds. They are a wonderful solution and can enable you to grow vegetables regardless of where you stay, even in climates that are only fit for seasonal planting. It is a great way to make gardening accessible even when you do not have the kind of setting that favors gardening.

Protection From Pets and Pests

Pets—especially dogs—and gardens do not always work well together. The same bedding where seedlings have just taken, earning your admiration, can quickly become a disappointing eyesore once your dog considered it an attraction for entirely different reasons. Yet, in my experience, pets are less likely to jump into raised garden beds. Of course, there is always the chance that a bigger animal will still jump into your beds and cause havoc, but in general, plants are far more protected in these beds as they serve as a deterrence.

Yet, it is not only our pets that sometimes have little understanding of the value of what we create. Rodents and other animals roaming the area at night can also tunnel their way through the soil to where your juicy carrots are waiting to be harvested. By adding wire cloth or even a solid base to raised beds, you can prevent these pests from getting into the soil and keep your produce safe. Just keep in mind that this is only a solution when it comes to higher gardens as the cloth or solid foundation will prevent roots from growing deep enough to ensure that your plants bear enough fruit.

Sometimes we can create damage in our own garden beds. When the beds are made on the soil surface, it is easy to step into them accidentally or you can even damage plants while walking by and rip or bend leaves with your shoes. You can also cause damage if you rely on a watering hose to hydrate the entire garden. Unless you are careful, you can end up damaging garden beds with the hose when you are watering. As raised beds are much higher than the surface, it is far less likely that these plants will sustain any of the above-mentioned damage.

Enjoy a Longer Growing Season

It is quite amazing to see how much warmer the soil is when it is lifted from the surface. During colder months, you might notice some frost on the surface of the ground all around the beds, but not on the surface. The same happens when it snows. The snowfall on the raised beds tends to melt much faster than the snow surrounding the boxes. This is simply because the smaller section of soil in the bed is not directly impacted by the temperature of the surrounding ground soil. The result is of course that you are able to enjoy a longer planting season in these boxes than when you have a normal vegetable garden in your backyard. It is also easy to cover the boxes to protect your crops from the most severe weather conditions.

The Solution to Muddy Messes

Another benefit of raised garden beds is that you will be less likely to have to deal with muddy messes in your garden. Some areas tend to get very wet during the rainy season and when you enter your vegetable garden, you may find that it has turned into one muddy pool. As raised beds are above the surface of the soil, they drain much faster than the surrounding ground soil and your plants will never be stuck in soil that is too moist for them to handle. You can improve this even more by filling these beds with soil that is great for drainage.

These are all great benefits to take into consideration when you are pondering what kind of garden you want to create at your home.

THE DISADVANTAGES OF RAISED GARDEN BEDS

While the number of benefits will always overshadow the disadvantages of raised garden beds, I felt it would only be fair to also give you an insight into what the drawbacks are of this kind of gardening.

It Can Be Expensive to Start Out

You may have already been wondering how much it would cost to start this type of garden as it can be a bit pricey. Maybe you already have some materials you can use to get you started, but it can also be that you need to buy everything that you need. The shopping list can become lengthy if you consider hosepipes, wood, or any other material for the boxes, the correct soil, seedlings or seeds, and mulch. However, once you have paid for all of the materials, you have settled most of the bill for your garden. While starting a garden in the soil may not be as expensive in the beginning, your continued expenses will eventually run up to be far higher than what you would pay to start a raised bed garden. This makes raised bed gardening the cheaper alternative over time.

You May Run Out of Space

What are you planning to plant? If you are going to produce mostly smaller crops like strawberries, carrots, beets or beans, or even peas, these boxes will offer enough space to do just that. However, if you want to grow pumpkins in your garden, you may run out of space unless you have very large boxes.

These Boxes Do Not Last Forever

Depending on how extreme the weather conditions are in your area, your boxes may need to be replaced from time to time. In most cases, the boxes are made of wood, and being a natural fiber, they do suffer damage from exposure. So, keep in mind that you will be able to maintain your boxes for many years, but at some point, you may have to gradually start to replace them.

They Are More Permanent

Now, I know that to some this may sound a little contradictory, but let me explain why it is not. You might decide to build a raised garden bed in a specific spot that appears to be ideal, but not long after, you might change your mind. It can be a bit of a problem as this would require more than just making the soil even again. In this case, a raised bed garden can be considered to be a more permanent fixture and for some gardeners, this may be a disadvantage.

You Are Restricted By Shape

Most raised garden beds have some kind of rectangular shape while you may also find a couple of round or oval-shaped ones. Depending on the surrounding area and what your plans are for the space, this can become limiting. Though, if you are constructing one, you are only limited by your imagination.

You May Need Some Handyman Skills (And Tools)

Most raised garden beds are constructed on the spot where you plan to keep them. So, you might need to have a little know-how of how to nail pieces of wood together. You may also need a drill and a saw and if you want to make it all look nice, perhaps a sander. So, essentially, even though you do not need to be the best handyman in the world, you may need to have some basic skills to ensure your raised beds can stand the test of time.

WRAPPING IT UP

Now you know where raised bed gardening originated and why I am so excited to share the guidelines and tips that will help you get started with your own garden and start producing fresh and healthy vegetables at your home.

Next, I will reveal some secrets of what you need to put inside your raised beds to ensure you enjoy optimal results.

2

IMPORTANCE OF GOOD SOIL PLUS FIVE SECRETS TO SUPERCHARGE YOUR GARDEN

There can be no life without soil and no soil without life; they have evolved together.

— CHARLES E. KELLOGG

Before you will be able to create a blend of healthy soil for the plants in your raised garden beds, you need to understand what healthy soil looks like.

WHAT IS HEALTHY SOIL?

Soil health plays a vital role to ensure that your plants bear optimal crops, no matter if you are growing flowers or vegetables. When I say optimal, I refer to both an abundance of produce but also flowers and vegetables that are of excellent quality. For example, if your soil is healthy, it increases the chances that your vegetables will be high in nutrients and healthier to eat.

That said, I am sure you wonder what the features of healthy soil are, and whether soil health is something that is visible to the eye. The short answer to the last part of the question is both yes and no. There are certain features of healthy soil that you will be able to see, but there are also attributes that you will only be able to determine by sending soil samples to be tested by a lab. I am not going to delve that deep into soil health since I think being able to judge the state of the soil or the plants you have in your raised garden beds just by looking at it should suffice.

To ensure you have healthy soil, you need to make sure that your raised garden beds are deep enough. I have already mentioned the preferred minimum height for these raised beds, but it is important to remember that deeper soil provides more room for root development.

Healthy soil offers great drainage. Soil that allows water to pool on top will drown the plant while water that runs straight through, will subsequently dry out the plant. The ideal soil has the ability to let the water slowly percolate through, allowing the root system to absorb the water and nutrients in the soil as needed.

While you do not want the soil to be too compacted, you can welcome a balanced level of soil aggregation. This means that you need to allow for some soil clumps in the bed, but it should never be compacted to form large masses of compacted soil. If this is the case, drainage, as well as root development, will suffer. Essentially, you want the soil to have good tilth and be loose but clumpy.

Healthy soil also has a rich brown color and is alive with organisms living in it. If you dig your fingers into the soil and find an earthworm, consider yourself lucky for these are an indication of healthy soil and while the worms stay there, you can be sure that the soil will remain in an optimal state for much longer.

HOW TO BUILD RAISED GARDEN BEDS WITH HEALTHY SOIL

One of the advantages of raised garden beds is that you have better quality control over the soil. There are a couple of steps you need to follow to get your soil into a healthy state. These steps are very similar to making deposits into your savings account. The math is simple, the more money you deposit, the more your money will draw interest and the higher your balance will be. Eventually, you will be able to make a withdrawal that will be well worth your efforts. However, far too many inexperienced—and sometimes experienced—gardeners tend to simply make withdrawals from their soil by harvesting one crop after the other without ever making deposits in the form of compost, fertilizers, or nutrients. If you only make withdrawals, your bank account will soon run empty and you will be left with nothing. I do not want your raised garden beds to ever get to such a state as it can take quite a bit of time for the soil to recover but, by following the next five steps, you will be able to avoid such a dire situation.

There are several ways to enrich the soil in your raised garden beds and each route you choose will have a different positive value to contribute to your garden. Yet, it does not matter in which way you add value to your soil, but rather that you do.

Compost

Adding compost is something that even those very new to gardening can identify as a way to enrich the value of their soil. But what does it entail and how can you do it right? The main reason why composting is widely known as a way to enrich any garden is that it is such a high-value deposit to make.

Compost is organic material that has been broken down. As time goes by, the microorganisms present in the compost break down the organic material, and you are left with a rich and nutritious way to increase the value of your soil. Through the breakdown process, the nutrients in the organic material become available to be absorbed again. Compost has the kind of texture that you want your soil to have to offer sufficient drainage. It is also loaded with good fungi and bacteria that contribute to the overall health of your soil and your plants.

As compost contains all you need to ensure a healthy garden, it is the best thing you can ever add to your soil. Adding compost will surely fix most problems you may experience with the soil or in your garden and therefore, adding enough compost to the soil when you fill your raised beds is essential.

Wood Chip Mulch

Next in line and almost as valuable as compost is mulch. As time goes by and the mulch breaks down, it will eventually also turn into compost, but even before it does, it already adds value to your soil by keeping weeds at bay. However, wood chips are only a single form of organic material and therefore offer a more limited contribution to the value of the soil in your garden. Thus, as compost consists of different types of organic material, the composition of nutrients it has to offer is far richer than what you will find in wood chip mulch alone. A simple example of this is that woodchip mulch contains quite a bit of carbon, but far less nitrogen, and if your soil needs nitrogen, this may not be the optimal way to address this deficiency. Wood chip mulch takes a long time to break down, but because of this, it is beneficial to the structure of your soil. Keep in mind that this is not the only type of mulch you can use. Any organic matter that takes a while to break down and through the process improves the structure of your soil and gradually adds nutrients can be a great mulching option.

Discarded Plant Parts

Every time you harvest, you are essentially taking away some of the nutrients in the soil. But you can also choose to leave some behind. For example, when you are harvesting, do not take the plant parts that might look a little off due to leaf damage or insect bites home only to discard them there. No, rather rip these off right there in your garden and add them to the soil. The term commonly used is "chop and drop." These parts will break down gradually and release the nutrients back into the ground. This supports good soil maintenance and ensures that the nutrient value remains higher for longer.

Leaving Plant Roots Behind

When you are harvesting from plants and they have reached the end of their lifespan, it is best not to uproot the entire plant by pulling it out of the soil. Instead, break the stem of the plant at the surface of the soil and leave the roots in the soil. You can do the same with plants that have died due to frost or any other reason. By leaving the old roots in the ground, you are improving the health of the soil as the roots are organic material that breaks down and adds nutrients—even though it is just a small amount—to the soil. As the roots form a network that traps air pockets, it helps to maintain great soil structure, keeping the soil loose but also airy. This is especially helpful if you are going to leave the soil for a bit before planting again but it is also only applicable to annuals. When it comes to perennials, you should not break down the plant as you are expecting to harvest from it yearly.

Bagged Soil

Bagged soil is the last resort and the deposit you can make to your garden that will make the smallest contribution to the soil quality. These bags are essentially filled with broken-down compost that has been sifted and there is often a lot of filler material added to it. The compost may be of great quality and be quite rich in nutrients, but the filler material with which it is diluted does not really contain any mentionable value. Considering that these bags come at quite a price, you would want to limit your usage of these bags as much as possible. So, when would you use them? When you need to fill up raised beds and do not have enough good soil and compost available yet.

TIPS TO IMPROVE THE QUALITY OF YOUR SOIL

Up until now, I have covered the basic steps that are necessary to ensure that the soil in your raised garden is of exceptional quality. But there are more things that you can do to ensure your plants have the optimal soil they deserve and that you enjoy the returns you desire from your garden. These are the tips I have learned over many years of working with my hands in the soil and tending to the plants in my raised garden beds.

Do Not Step on It!

Do not step on your soil. Do not step into your raised beds as every time you do, you effectively squeeze the air out of the soil and compact it. Soil is alive and you should keep that in mind whenever you are working in your beds. Just as you will not step onto anything else that is alive, you should also not step onto your soil when you expect to have healthy plants that bear great crops. Consider this when you initially plan and set up your raised garden beds for they need to be in a place and of a size that allows you to easily reach every part of the box without having to put pressure on the surface.

Wet Soil

I think it might even be clearer to say, you should not work in wet soil. Sure, working in wet soil is messy, but messy clothes can be washed with ease, and getting air back into your soil is difficult. It requires a lot of work to get air back in between the soil particles. When you work with wet soil, you are effectively agitating the soil particles that are surrounded by water and this pushes the air to the surface and out of the soil. The test to see if the soil is too wet to work with is to simply take a handful of soil and squeeze it. If water comes out of the soil, leave it for now as it is still too wet for gardening.

Soil Likes Coffee Too

Are you a coffee drinker? Or, perhaps even someone who simply cannot seem to function early in the morning until they have their first cup of coffee? Well, your soil also likes coffee so do not discard your leftover coffee grounds. Coffee has naturally high acidity levels and will help you to either bring the soil into balance if it has high alkaline levels or it can make the soil more acidic, which some plants love. The most practical option here is to dump your coffee grinds in a container and simply scatter it across your beds when it is full.

NO MORE EXCUSES GET OUT AND GROW | 41

Hay Can Do Wonders for Your Garden

This tip is especially helpful to those who have the space for a couple of animals in their yards. Whether it is bunnies, goats, or any other animal that require hay bedding, you can use the dirty hay that you usually chuck out when cleaning up their mess as a brilliant way to improve the quality of your soil. The hay will break down, even if it is already moldy, and the mess that your animals leave on this hay is loaded with minerals that will only enhance the quality of the soil.

HOW TO OVERCOME DEFICIENCIES

When your garden continues to underperform and you have added all you can think of, it may be necessary to have your soil tested. It is often the case that soil has all it needs but lacks sufficient nitrogen, simply because it is the one element that very easily escapes from the soil.

Lab results will tell you what your soil needs, but as you grow more familiar with gardening and the conditions you need to look out for, you will reach a point where you will be able to identify what is lacking simply by looking at how your plants behave. Gardening is a process that demands greater awareness and by being mindful when you spend time in your garden, you will become more familiar with the soil and plant needs you may have to address.

Nitrogen

As I already mentioned, nitrogen escapes easily from the soil. If this is the cause of your concerns, and you already have peas growing in your garden, be sure to work the plants into the soil after you have harvested them. Peas are naturally high in nitrogen and will bring the nitrogen content up to a healthy level again.

Potassium

If you experience regular cramps or muscle spasms, it is usually due to a potassium deficiency for which the natural cure is to eat more bananas. When your soil lacks potassium, you can address the problem by working the ash from a wood fire into it. Any ash from a wood-burning stove or fireplace will do the trick and help to replenish the much-needed potassium.

44 | G. GREY

Phosphorus

One way to address a phosphorus deficiency is through bone meal, which has high levels of the mineral. However, bone meal can be smelly and may not be something you would like to work with, especially if you do not want to use any animal products in your garden. In this case, you can also address a phosphorous deficiency by adding rock phosphate.

Magnesium

As soil is alive, the deficiencies it suffers are very similar to what people experience. You can add Epsom salt to the beds and work it into the soil to bring the magnesium in your soil back to a healthy level.

Calcium

While we need calcium for strong teeth and bones, the soil needs calcium to ensure healthy crops. Calcium deficiency is something that can prevent your plants from bearing the crops you desire as you may experience a low yield or even crops of poor quality. There are three things you can add to your soil to correct this situation, they might be quite unusual but they work. Oyster shells are a great way to increase calcium. It helps to break the shells down as finely as possible to make it easier to work them into the soil. Limes are another great source of calcium for soil and so is powdered milk. The latter is probably not that surprising as we rely on dairy products to increase our own calcium levels.

FIVE SECRETS TO SUPERCHARGE YOUR GARDEN

Soil care also includes more than just maintaining healthy soil. There may be times when you want to give your garden that added energy—a boost to get it to perform optimally. So, here are my five top tips to boost your soil health and improve the state of your plants and crops. You will be able to buy any of these five solutions at your local gardening shop or online.

Biochar

The value of biochar was discovered when researchers explored the impact of climate change and how it impacts the carbon levels in the air and soil (Return-Project, 2015). Studies on ancient civilizations in the Amazon have shown how people used to enrich their soil by adding charcoal to it. This soil, which has a black tone, compared to the yellow soil in the surroundings, is called *terra preta*. It was found that this carbon-rich soil withdraws more carbon from the air and can reduce the increased level of carbon gasses caused by burning fossil fuels and global warming.

Biochar, therefore, restores the carbon levels in the soil. By adding it to your soil, you can increase your crop yields several times and improve the quality of your plants. Biochar is basically the charcoal left over from wood burning but differs from the charcoal and ashes you will find in your fireplace. To get nutrient-rich biochar, the wood needs to be burned in ovens that contain little oxygen to ensure that it contains a sufficient carbon content. When adding it to your soil, you should also activate it by mixing it with quality compost in a ratio of 1:1 or, soaking it in compost tea for 24 hours.

Adding biochar to your soil will improve the soil's ability to hold water. Globally, urbanization has created a need for development on an immense scale. This level of development impacts the soil all around us and it is often the case that surface water will only run off instead of soaking into the soil. Adding biochar will address the water runoff in your garden. Yet, it is not only water retention that improves but also the soil's ability to retain nutrients. Biochar also contributes by creating a more stable environment for the microorganisms that live in the soil, keeping your soil in a healthy state. Due to these three factors, it is a wonderful addition to your raised beds to improve your yield. Lastly, adding biochar to your soil also benefits the environment as it fixes the carbon levels in the soil thus helping to decrease the carbon content in our air, something that is getting out of hand due to the immense amount of carbon dioxide we release into the atmosphere every time we burn fossil fuels.

Mycorrhizae

Mycorrhizae are naturally present around plants below the surface of the soil. It is a type of fungus, and although it is a microorganism, it can grow to be similar in size to a mushroom. Truffles, for example, are one kind of edible mushroom produced by mycorrhizae. These organisms form an underground network, which helps plants to connect with each other. The relationship between plants and mycorrhizae is therefore mutually beneficial. They help plants to absorb nutrients more effectively as they connect to and become an extension of the plant roots, allowing the plant to absorb as much as 700 times more nutrients than before ("The Benefits of Using Mycorrhizae in the Garden," 2021). Mycorrhizae also help to break down the soil and organic matter, a process that releases nutrients into the soil and improves its structure. The result is more nutrient-rich soil and better yields. But plants also contribute to this relationship as they break down sugars into a form that the mycorrhizae can absorb and as the fungi never have any exposure to the sun, they rely on plants to gain access to the benefits of sunlight.

Rhizobacteria

Would you like to have soil that ensures better absorption of macro and micronutrients, beds where organic matter breaks down faster, and where your plants are safe from abiotic stress, all while you contribute to a healthier horticultural environment? These are some of the benefits your garden can enjoy when you add rhizobacteria to the garden beds. But what is it exactly? You most likely know that bacteria are tiny organisms that are present everywhere. You will find bacteria in soil, water, the air, and even in your body. There are good and bad bacteria, but rhizobacteria are good bacteria that contribute to plant health and wellness and therefore when you add it to your soil, you give your beds a boost that will increase their yield.

Worm Castings

Worm castings consist of worm manure in the shape of a worm. Earthworms are the ones most widely found in soil, but they do prefer certain types of soil above others and they choose to live in healthy soil that contains enough water. These worms eat the organic material in the soil and their digestive systems break it down to form worm castings, increasing the nutrient levels and uptake in the soil.

Your plants need four things to flourish: quality soil, nutrients to absorb from the soil, sufficient moisture, and air. Worm castings increase all four of these. As the worms live and move underneath the surface, they create small air pockets and loosen the consistency of the soil which helps the plant roots and root systems to grow stronger. Stronger root systems ensure that plants can absorb more moisture and nutrients delivering strong and healthy plants, bigger crops, and better-tasting produce. These castings also protect your plants against certain pests. Worm castings contain an enzyme called chitinase, which dissolves chitin, the substance many pests like whiteflies are made of. The worm castings leave the enzyme in the soil and the surrounding plants absorb the enzyme. Now the enzyme is present in the plant sap and when these insects suck the plant sap, the chitinase dissolves them, keeping your garden pest-free ("Castings - a Magic Spell for Soil Health," n.d.). Essentially, worm castings contribute to the soil by improving every element your plants depend on. An added benefit is that you can buy worm castings from your garden center if you don't want to have a worm vermiculture bin.

Nitrogen Fixing Plants

Nitrogen is naturally present in soil and, as it supports the growth of green leaves improving photosynthesis, your plants will always need it. It is also a core building block of plant proteins. Soil can become depleted of nitrogen due to a range of factors, but you can improve this condition by planting nitrogen-fixing plants. These plants absorb nitrogen from the air and put it into the soil. Various plants can help increase the nitrogen levels in your soil and you can either plant them in your garden boxes on a rotational level, between your existing plants, or on the edges of the boxes. These plants include legumes and certain shrubs, and the following are my preferred options for raised garden beds:

- green beans
- peas
- lupins
- white and red clover
- wood, American, or tufted vetch

Healthy soil is vital when you aim to have great yields and healthy, great-tasting produce. You can do a lot to ensure your raised garden beds provide your plants with an optimal environment to flourish. Next, we are going to start planning your garden and explore all you need to consider while doing so.

PLANNING YOUR GARDEN

I like gardening—it is a place where I find myself when I need to lose myself.

— ALICE SEBOLD

Earlier on I mentioned that one of the disadvantages of raised garden beds is that they are relatively permanent. This is already one good reason why you would want to make sure that you plan your garden well in advance. Moving raised garden beds can be a very difficult and dirty job. So a few minutes of planning will save you hours of heavy labor.

Then, you probably also want your garden to be practical and effective, and as it is likely situated right next to your home on your property, you want it to look nice as well. It should have a kind of visual appeal that adds value to your property.

In this chapter, I will share all you need to know when starting out with your raised bed garden. These planning tips will help reduce any potential anxiety you have and guide you along when you feel like you might be in over your head. So, do not worry—you have got this. I will also share tips on how you can improve your planning around any existing beds if you have already started on your journey, but have not quite settled in yet.

PLANNING TIPS

The first step you need to take is finding the perfect spot to set up your raised beds, do this even before you gather all the timber and tools from the shed to start building your boxes.

Stand back for a moment and look at your property. What do you see? How much space do you have available? Which area(s) would be best complimented by the boxes you have in mind? These are all important questions, but I believe the primary determining factor is whether the spot you are considering gets sufficient morning sun. Plants need the sun to grow, but the afternoon sun tends to be much harsher than the morning sun. The sun's rays during the latter part of the day can burn your plants and dry out the soil very quickly. Harsh direct sunlight also increases the heat of the soil, making it harder for plants to grow. Remember that the soil in garden boxes is already a bit warmer than the soil on the surface of your garden. This is considered to be a benefit, but you also need to keep in mind that wherever you set up the garden boxes, your plants need to be protected throughout the year, regardless of the season.

What can you do if the space you have available only gets afternoon sun? Try to add shade to your garden boxes. You can always add more shade but you cannot add more sunlight. So, the only real place that garden boxes will not bring you the yields you are hoping for, would be severely shaded areas that get almost no sunlight.

Other features you should be looking for are a space where the surface is already relatively level and one with a nearby water source. You would preferably want a tap in close vicinity to make watering with a hose easy. Also, consider how well the soil in that area drains. The soil should not be too dry, but too much water, or even worse, water that does not drain fast enough out of your garden beds, is also not something you want.

Once you have the perfect spot—well, it does not really have to be perfect, you are after all stepping into nature, but it should at least be relatively decent and suitable for what you have in mind—you need to measure the size of the area. Determine the length and width of the area you plan to utilize for your garden.

The size of the area will determine how many boxes you will be able to set up. Now may be the best time to turn to the drawing board. Drawing an image of your garden and the size of your boxes on the same scale will help give you a visual image of what you can fit into the space and how big your boxes can be. I do not recommend that you make your boxes any larger than 4 ft across, because you need to be able to move around the box and still reach the middle from any side. You can also place some of your boxes against a wall, but if you do, these boxes should never be more than 2 ft wide, otherwise, you will have to press onto the surface of the soil to get to the deeper ends which will compact the soil.

You have complete freedom when it comes to the length of the boxes. While longer boxes may look nice, just keep in mind that you still have to move around them to work in the raised beds from all sides.

Just as important as the size of the boxes, is the width of the pathways you leave open between them. You need to give yourself enough space to move around easily without bumping into or damaging the plants that are right on the edge of the boxes or even hanging over the sides. The ideal width in this regard is three or maybe even four feet if you have enough space to play around a bit. I typically leave enough room to get a wheelbarrow in and out. You will thank me when you are adding compost or soil to your beds.

This may take a bit of time, but planning your garden on paper is far less labor-intensive than moving around heavy pieces of wood later on. Having a physical plan in your hands will also help guide you when you mark out the exact spot and determine the best size for the boxes. But even if you have a plan on paper, bear in mind that when you are back in your garden it may not work as you have envisioned it.

So, I recommend that you mark out the size of your boxes and maybe use cheap fabric to cut out the exact shapes. Then lay them down in the spots that you have indicated on your plan and spend a bit of time in the space. How does it make you feel? Are you wasting any space or could you perhaps fit in more boxes? Or, maybe you have been a bit over-optimistic about the number of boxes you planned to fit in and have to rethink your entire plan as the space now feels over-crowded.

Do not proceed with cutting the wood or making the boxes until you are completely sure that you are not over or under-utilizing the space you have. Look at the markers you have placed in the area; if you feel like you are on the edge of making the place feel too full, it will be better to replan your garden instead. If it feels almost too full when you only have markers on the surface, it will surely feel like too much when you have the boxes in. Depending on the size of your garden, you may want to add some vertical elements as well. These will make the space fill up much faster. You need to be sure that you are not including too many boxes, so keep all these factors in mind, before proceeding to make your raised bed boxes.

One more feature to consider is where you could install some vertical elements in your garden for both aesthetic and practical purposes. These give a sense of height and variety to an area filled with boxes of the same height and shape, but they also provide support to plants that grow higher than others. Plants like peas that like to attach to higher surfaces will also appreciate vertical elements. The most common type of vertical element you will find in raised bed gardens is a trellis. Trellises do not block off the area, make it look smaller, or more crowded than what it is, nor do they block out the sunlight and they can be made to look very pretty. One last point to remember is to be creative and have fun during your planning process!

BED BOX TIPS

Before making any decision regarding what material you are going to use for your raised bed boxes, take a moment to consider what are you going to use these boxes for. Even though the options might be limited, there are still some choices as to what you can use to construct the beds. Some gardeners may prefer to use stone, while others like to use metal. However, most boxes are made out of wood. Pinewood boxes may be cheaper to make, but they will not last as long as boxes made of a harder kind of wood, like redwood. In the next chapter, I will discuss different box ideas in greater detail.

What should you do when your budget only allows for cheaper materials but you would still like to enjoy a longer-lasting garden? Start by building your garden in segments. You do not have to build the complete garden in one go, and you will have your plan to refer back to when you have money to invest in the garden again at a later stage. I believe that a couple of good quality boxes—even as few as one, two, or perhaps three—is a better investment to make than installing a large number of boxes made of cheap materials that will force you to redo your garden soon after. Installing your garden in phases will also help you to decide if your initial plan was good enough to see through. You may want to make minor changes to your beds before adding more. Remember that your garden should become a space where you like spending your time, so be sure that you are truly happy with every part you add before proceeding to the next. For example, see what the space feels like once you have installed the boxes but have not added the soil yet. When the boxes are still empty, they can be moved relatively easily. Thus, spend enough time in the space so that you know you are 100% happy with the placement before filling them up.

Installing the boxes is another vital part of the process. It may not bother you if they are not evenly spaced at first, or if you have not leveled them before adding the soil, but believe me, after looking at these boxes for weeks, or months, these small inconsistencies can become quite a big deal—even if you do not consider yourself to be a perfectionist. Rather invest the time and effort at the start to check that all boxes are level and that pathways are equally distributed between boxes.

Watering systems vary from garden to garden. You might be planning to water your plants by hand with a hose, or perhaps you have an idea of a water system that you would like to install in every box for effortless watering. If you are planning on the latter, the best time to install such a system is while the boxes are still empty. It is easy to install water pipes to run inside the boxes, hiding the pipes from plain sight. This is not a necessary step, but it will make your garden look much neater and more well-kept.

Allow me to quickly add that installing water beds is an effective way to ensure your beds have sufficient water. These are a network of equally distributed water pipes that you can lay on top of the surface of the bed. The network of pipes is then connected to a water source and by opening the tap, your raised beds can get sufficient water with minimal effort. If you have not considered yet how you are going to water your garden, I urge you to explore watering beds in greater detail to determine whether it is the right solution for you.

It is only once you have all of these boxes ticked, that you are ready to fill your beds with quality soil.

PLANTING TIPS

Before you actually start planting in the boxes, you may want to return to your garden plan—or draw an alternative one indicating the boxes that you have already installed and what type of sunlight each box gets. When you are planting, make sure to put the plants that love sunlight in these lighter spots and those that are more sensitive to sunlight in shaded areas.

Moisture content in boxes also plays a role in where you will be planting what. Typically, the outer parts of garden boxes are drier than the center. Water drains easier in these parts while the core of the box better retains moisture. Therefore, when drawing your planting plan, try to plant according to the moisture content in each part of the box.

Two of the most important tips to consider remain, including that you have to plant things that will grow well in your climate. Later on, I will discuss hardiness zones, but it may also be helpful to get a plant guide to know what plants do well in your climate and which ones you should not even bother with. Another determining factor is what vegetables you prefer to have in your garden. Ask yourself what vegetables your family eats the most. It does not make sense to plant things that you do not even like to eat.

Are you considering trying companion planting? If so, it will definitely impact your planting plan. Companion planting refers to the fact that certain plants prefer to grow close to specific other plants and when planted close enough to each other, they help each other to perform and produce a better yield. Tomatoes—something you will find in almost every raised garden—are probably one of the most popular companion plants. Tomato plants grow exceptionally well when you have basil, cucumber, or even marigolds in your garden. I expand more on companion planting in chapter five to give you a great foundation in this regard.

Wait a minute! If you are planting a vegetable garden, why would you want to include plants like marigolds? Marigolds are only one example of a variety of flowers that will contribute to bringing out the best in your vegetable garden. Some plants that are essentially flowers are also known for their use in the kitchen and for keeping pests away. Exploring what flowers you can add to your garden can be another exciting side adventure in your gardening journey. Just as there are plants that do well when they are planted close to each other, there are also plants that do not like to have each other as neighbors. Looking at tomatoes again, you will find that they do not like to be close to cabbage. If you have these plants next to each other, you can anticipate a much smaller yield than what you expected. How will you know what plants to put next to each other? Simply compile a list of all you would like to grow and then a quick online search will provide you with all you need to know when completing your planting plan.

Another great planting tip is to divide your box into blocks of a square foot each. If you have opted to install a watering system, the pipes are likely already providing you with these outlines—depending on the type of watering system you have chosen of course. When you divide your box like this, you get smaller blocks that will prevent you from planting too many plants in one box or planting them too close to each other. Each plant you choose to grow in your raised garden beds requires a specific amount of space. So, when you have a grid to work on, it makes it easier to get these spaces right and it is especially helpful if you plan to start your garden by planting seeds. All seed packets provide planting information and indicate how far apart you need to plant seeds making planting them in this grid really easy.

Plan your planting in such a manner that you can reuse certain parts of your boxes in one season. For example, plants that grow very quickly and have a short time frame between planting and harvesting open up the soil space for other plants with short growth periods, or something that does well later on in the season, or even plants that are not seasonal at all. You can also use these fast-growing plants for succession planting. If you know that a specific plant only requires a small time frame within the planting season, then plant different batches a couple of weeks apart. This will mean that you will have fresh produce to pick over a longer period, rather than harvesting a lot of one thing for a short time.

Another quick tip is to label your beds. This does not require much material or effort, but can help remind you of what you planted where, especially if you plant from seeds. We often think that we will remember exactly what we planted where, but you might end up changing your mind last minute and since seeds take a while to grow into recognizable plants, you may completely lose track of what is already in the soil.

A COUPLE OF GENERAL TIPS

These tips are not linked to any specific phase of the planting process, but they are helpful in general.

Keep a journal. Get a gardening book and keep a record of what you have planted where, how well it did, and how large the yield was. Make notes every planting season of what you would like to do better or differently when the next planting season arrives. Such a gardening book will form the foundation of your knowledge that can expand every month, season, and year. Capturing your progress, problems, and challenges will give you a good reference of any problem areas in your garden that you need to address.

Your gardening book is also a place where you can capture a wish list of plants you would like to have in your garden in the future. Or, it can serve as a reminder of plants you do not want to try again as they just do not work well in your area.

Gardening is also very weather dependent. Capture the weather of your planting season to have a record to revert to during the next season. Your gardening journal can therefore provide you with all you need to know to be better prepared next time. Remember the key to success is to do more of that which worked well and less of that which did not go as planned.

Even though I have said that a flat surface is best for your beds, it may be that you have no choice but to build them on a slight slope. If this is the case, remember to rake these beds regularly to even out the soil. Gravity will pull the water and gradually the soil to the lowest end of your box and therefore it can become a saturated spot. So, every time you harvest from the box and start to prepare it for your next planting session, be sure to rake all the soil back up first so that you have the closest to a level surface you can get.

Planting your first garden can be a time filled with nervous anticipation. After all, you have invested time and money in getting your garden to this point and you probably have dreams and visualizations of what it would look like in your mind, and perhaps also a fear of failure. Have a little faith in nature and in yourself. Trust the process and know that if you have done your share, the rest will happen without any effort.

4

IDEAS FOR RAISED BEDS PLUS FIVE LOW-COST BEDS

Whatever good things we build end up building us.

— JIM ROHN

Up until now, I have mainly mentioned wooden plant boxes as this is the most popular choice of material for planter beds. However, wood can be expensive, especially if you want to use quality wood that will offer longevity to your garden. In this chapter, I want to open an entire world of possibilities for materials you can choose, and you will see that, while many people prefer to use wood, it is not your only option.

WOOD BOARDS

Copyright Jamie Hooper | Dreamstime.com

Wood, being the popular choice, is probably the best place to start and even when you decide to use wood, you still have a couple of options to choose from.

Wood boards can be a great option if you want to give your raised garden beds a classic appeal. Building garden beds from wood requires access to equipment like a drill, nail gun, and a circular saw, which means you need to have the skills to operate these tools safely and know how to work with wood. If you want the option to dismantle your boxes again in the future, it would be best to use screws instead of nails as you will be able to easily unscrew the parts. When purchasing wood for gardening boxes, always buy untreated wood. Treated wood may last longer but is loaded with chemicals that will release into the soil over time which you do not want as it will negatively affect your plants. As the wood is untreated, you will have to invest in a good sealer to protect the wood from water damage. Linseed oil is a great choice for a natural sealant.

To proceed, you will need to measure the lengths of wood you have to cut and this is where you will need some skills. Make sure that you have got all your measurements correct before cutting. Once you have all your pieces cut to size, you can nail or screw them into the box shape. By adding wooden supports in the corners of the box shape, you will ensure that your boxes remain intact for longer.

Once the box is complete, give it a nice coat of linseed oil, both on the inside and the outside. When the oil has drawn into the wood, you are ready to place your box in position and start adding your soil.

WOODEN TIERED BEDS

These might be a bit more expensive than the previous option as a lot of work is already done for you. You can get these tiered beds from various gardening shops or online and they are available in different sizes. All you need to do is to unbox and assemble the parts and you are ready to go.

WOOD FRAMES COUPLED WITH STEEL ROOFING

Copyright Matthew J Roberson 2023

I must say that I quite fancy these boxes as they have a rustic/modern appeal and can add a special touch to your garden. You would need wood beams to build the frame but instead of using wood throughout, you use steel roofing for the side panels. While this used to be a more affordable option, the price of building materials has spiked over recent years and this is no longer the most affordable way of building raised garden beds.

Yet, they are still practical and attractive and can be a relatively quick build.

The tools you would need are the lumber and sheets, coiled straps, linseed oil to protect the wood, screws, and the power tools you would need to get the job done. In this case, it would be a grinder, circular saw, drill, square, and screws.

CONCRETE BLOCKS

Copyright Vaivirga | Dreamstime.com

Building a garden with cinder blocks may be easier than building it with wood. You will need less equipment and also do not need to have any special skills as it is not that hard to stack rows of cinder blocks on top of each other with mortar in between. These blocks create a robust solution to keep the soil from being washed away.

As you are building a structure, you would need to create a foundation first. Therefore, once you have marked where you want to build the raised beds, you can start digging out a foundation. Considering the nature of such a built structure and how permanent this option is, it would be best to do proper planning—as described in chapter three—to ensure that you have got your garden layout correct.

Once the foundation has been laid, it needs to settle for at least a couple of days. Only then, will you be able to continue building the next rows of blocks on top of it. Depending on the size of the blocks you use, you may have to add about three of four layers to get the correct height for your planter boxes.

STEEL BEDS

Copyright Hollyharryoz | Dreamstime.com

Steel beds can be a cheaper option compared to wood and—best of all—requires no handyman skills as you buy these completely pre-made. Steel beds for raised garden beds are available in various sizes and you can find options that suit your available space perfectly. Shop around before buying these beds as there are several features you need to consider. A quality steel bed is made of a steel substrate core, covered with a zinc alloy coating, and the last layer of protection against moisture and adverse weather conditions is USDA Certified paint. The latter is important, as with the treatments used on wood, the toxins in ordinary paint are also released into the soil over time, affecting the quality of your soil and plants. Therefore, pay a little more to be sure that your garden is kept safe from toxic materials.

HARDIE-PLANK SIDING BOARDS

Hardie-Planks are an affordable option to use for garden beds and they are already treated against rot. As the surface of your garden bed will get exposed to a lot of moisture and the living organisms in the soil, you will need to use materials that will not rot away. While these planters still have a wooden structure, the sides are made of Hardie-Plank that has been treated but contains minimal chemicals. The two greatest benefits of this option are that it is more affordable and it looks really good when done.

The reason why this is such an effective option is that Hardie-Plank is made of fiber cement. The material is naturally protected against rot as it is intended for outside use. Bugs are also not a problem and therefore you do not need to apply any treatment to protect your garden beds. But one factor that you need to keep in mind is that these boards bend, making it a less secure option to hold the box in shape. You can easily overcome this problem by adding wooden supports along the side to keep the board—and your raised bed—in place.

CONCRETE PAVER BEDS

Concrete pavers make beautiful neat beds. These beds offer a low-maintenance solution as the concrete will last a very long time regardless of the conditions it has to endure. The best way to give these paver beds stability is to bury them about half an inch to one inch in the soil. This will secure the bottom half of the box while you can secure the top half with a wooden frame that you simply screw together and slide over the top to keep the pavers together firmly. If you want an even more secure box, you can add construction adhesive or mortar between the pavers, but if you pack them close together, this may not even be necessary. This kind of raised bed box can easily be disassembled and moved while it will stay secured for many years to come.

COMPOSITE DECK BEDS

You can buy composite decking at most hardware stores. These are made of a lightweight material that is specifically designed to endure adverse weather conditions, and while they are usually installed horizontally to make decks, you can also use decking strips to make long-lasting garden beds.

Once you have cut the pieces to the desired lengths, you can start to assemble your box, either by nailing or screwing them together, or by using angle aluminum to hold the corners together more securely. If you choose the latter option, I suggest that you leave the pieces a little longer to create a spike-like shape that will go into the soil and keep the box securely in place. Building this kind of box offers you the choice to decide how complex or simple you want to make the design. Obviously, the more complex you go the more tools and skills you will need.

GABION BEDS

Not sure what Gabion beds are? Gabion beds are essentially beds that have a wired frame holding a whole lot of stones together. Now, I do not recommend these as a DIY solution as getting the wireframes shaped correctly and neatly can be a real pain and you cannot just use any kind of wire. Packing the stones densely enough to provide a secure frame that keeps the soil in place also requires a specific technique. However, if you can find someone to install these for you, it will add a wonderful visual appeal to your garden. This is also a more permanent option than some of the others I have mentioned so far.

These are not only beautiful to look at and to have in your garden, but they also offer a combination of durability and natural appeal. Gabion beds provide a greater sense of variety when it comes to shape and size as these frames can be made to suit your exact requirements. They can be a more expensive option, but if you are willing to pay a bit more at the start, you will most likely enjoy savings later on as there will be no need for maintenance.

SPLIT LOG BEDS

You will hardly find a bed option that is more affordable or quick and easy to make than split log beds. You only need hardware cloth that is long enough to shape the outer edge of the raised bed. It is best to choose an option that is wide enough to create the height you would like for your garden bed sides. Then, you will also need screws and split logs.

Wear gloves when taking on this project as the hardware cloth can be harsh on your hands. Start by laying out the hardware cloth so that you can measure the length you need. Once you have cut this, you can shape the hardware cloth to form a circle shape. Use wire to tie the ends together to form a circle and keep it in place.

You may want to protect the logs from the moisture and bugs in the soil as these logs are completely raw. You can use recycled compost bags for this layer. The best way to secure this plastic layer is to place it between the hardware cloth and the logs and put a screw into the wood from the inside through the plastic. The trick with these beds is to find logs that fit well next to each other as you do not want large gaps between the logs. You can use thick logs and split them in half and then place the flat side against the wire, use thinner logs and keep them intact, or combine different logs to add a natural and rustic feeling to your bed. Once you are done, go around on the outside and put another screw from this side into the bed. This will give you a secure raised garden bed that will keep the soil just where you want it to be.

DIY LOG BED

This is a labor-intensive option but it does create an amazing natural look. I do not recommend taking this project on alone as it requires some heavy lifting and you may need an extra hand to hold the logs as you operate the tools. That said, you will need specific tools, such as a chainsaw, and some woodwork skills.

These beds are made of larger logs that are stacked in layers on top of each other. Before stacking the logs, you will have to cut half-moon shapes into them so that each log fits precisely into the shape you have cut out of the log beneath and below it. This will keep the logs in position and allow you to layer the logs perfectly. If you have access to logs or have some trees that need to be cut down, it can be a great way to recycle wood, but this may not be the best option for most gardeners.

THE MOST AFFORDABLE ALTERNATIVES

It can be extremely frustrating if you are keen on starting your raised garden beds—as you should be of course—but just do not have the finances available for the material you need to build the beds. If this is where you find yourself, then I have good news: Raised garden beds do not have to be enclosed. They are merely longer lasting and more secure if they are. Yet, there are plenty of gardeners who choose not to have these structures in their gardens but still use raised garden beds for all their crops. How do they do it? Let us see.

Non-Enclosed Raised Beds

This method works well if the area in your yard that you want to transform into a raised bed garden is completely open. It would require that you simply level the soil and create your beds by forming heaps of healthy soil. If you have lots of weeds in the specific area you may first need to lay down a layer of cardboard and then create heaps of soil on top of the cardboard. The cardboard layer will protect your garden from weeds taking over and as cardboard is a biodegradable material, it will eventually disintegrate and become part of the soil.

Although this is a much cheaper option, it requires more regular maintenance as you may have to push the soil back to the top quite often. Watering is really the greatest risk to these beds for if it is not done carefully, the running water will take the soil with it. So, you will have to water the plants carefully, especially if they have not yet developed strong root systems to keep the soil in place. You can also place wood or logs to form an edge around the soil as it will offer at least some protection to keep it more securely in place.

Wattle Weaving Beds

Wattle weaving is an ancient technique used to create fences. For this, you would need to plant support poles in the shape of your raised garden. You can either use thin poles bought at your local timber supplier or other pieces of wood you have collected while looking for the longer pieces you plan to use for the wattle weaving. It all depends on how cost-effective you want to make your beds and how you want them to look once you are done.

84 | G. GREY

Copyright Halelujah | Dreamstime.com

For wattle weaving, you need branches that are very supple and can easily be weaved through the support poles you have planted to create the edge of your garden bed. It is a simple technique of putting the longer supple pieces in front of one pole and then going past the back of the next pole and then back to the front. Once you have added one of these branches, you can weave in the next in an alternating pattern, in other words, when the previous branch went around the pole at the back, the next would do so in front. When you have a couple of these weaved in, push it all down and continue adding branches until you have a weaved layer that is at the height you would like your bed to be.

This is a cheaper technique as there is no need for tools and you can collect most of the materials in your surroundings, depending on where you live. However, it is a labor-intensive option and it does require patience to get the job done. As this wood is also untreated and unprotected, it may not last as long.

Pallet Beds

Copyright Bernd Kelichhaus | Dreamstime.com

Pallets are extremely versatile and can be used to make furniture and all kinds of creative projects. It is also a great material for raised garden beds. One suggestion is to place them flat on the soil surface and fill them up with soil. Another suggestion is to remove some of the planks to widen the spaces between the slats or leave them just the way they are and plant in these spaces.

Another way would be to stack them in a triangle shape and then secure them in position. Fill these pallets with soil and plant your plants in the open spaces between the slats. Pallet beds add a rustic look to your garden and they work especially well when planting smaller plants like strawberries or herbs.

Hügelkultur Beds

Copyright Elmar Gubisch | Dreamstime.com

Hügelkultur beds are wonderfully exciting and were first created in Germany ("Hügelkultur: The Ultimate Raised Garden Beds," n.d.). When you look at these beds from afar, they look like small soil mountains that are covered with plants. These soil mountains are supported by wooden logs that are buried throughout the inside. So, to make your raised garden bed this way, you need to place several logs in position. Then cover the logs to form a sufficient layer of soil on top so that plants can grow in the soil. Give it a try. As these beds have wood at their core, they are a completely natural option offering outstanding drainage and you can continue to make them larger as time goes by. The wood core also retains moisture and is a good choice in arid regions. You do not need to buy anything to start such a bed and they offer a great natural appeal.

Straw Raised Beds

Straw can be used as a protective cover on the surface of all gardens, as part of compost, and as the edges of your raised garden beds. This natural material contains many nutrients and the older these straw sides become the more they turn into compost. Straw beds are affordable, easy to assemble, and look pretty in the garden. They are also a far less permanent option as it is easy to take these beds apart and you will have plenty of straw to work into your garden.

For every challenge you may face along your journey in creating raised garden beds, there is a range of solutions to pick from that best suit your situation and needs. Now that we have covered everything you need to know about the preparation of the perfect garden, we can shift our focus to planting. Even though I have already given a bird's eye view of planting, we are now going to dive much deeper into this topic.

UNLOCK THE SECRETS TO A THRIVING RAISED BED GARDEN

"The glory of gardening: hands in the dirt, head in the sun, heart with nature. To nurture a garden is to feed not just the body, but the soul."

— ALFRED AUSTIN

At the start of this book, I mentioned how surprised people are when I tell them that gardening can improve their quality of life *and* their lifespan.

Human beings are meant to be in nature. Studies by Cornell University researchers have shown that spending just 10 minutes in nature enables people to feel happier and less physically and mentally stressed.

One thing many people don't talk about too often, however, is what an inherently sociable activity it can be. Those who garden alongside friends and family members know that this life-giving hobby unites people, gives them a common goal to work towards, and gives older and younger gardeners alike a vital sense of responsibility.

I explained how my own love for gardening was instilled by my mother's magical ability to grow practically anything! Throughout my many travels, I also came across a myriad of people who shared their practices with me. I adapted many of the tips they taught me to the climate conditions where I live, and am so grateful for all the green-thumbed sages I met along the way.

Like them, I chose to guide and help others learn and sharpen their skills at gardening. It fulfills me deeply to share strategies that enable others to make the most of their climate, budget, and available space. In the end, we motivate and inspire each other to keep ourselves grounded to nature.

From Martha Stewart to Snoop Dogg, Jake Gyllenhaal to Michelle Obama… so many famous people are choosing gardening as a way to get closer to nature and get their families more excited about consuming healthy, home-grown produce.

You may not have the same media access as these celebrities. However, if gardening has changed your life for the better, and you have found this book helpful, spread the word.

By leaving a review of this book on Amazon, you'll motivate other readers to discover the joy of biting into a fresh, crunchy vegetable grown in their own garden.

Simply by telling them how this book enlightened you and what they can expect to find inside, you'll empower them with all the information they need to create a beautiful, vibrant raised bed garden. You will also help others supercharge their current gardens with ideal plant profiles for their hardiness zone.

Thank you for your support. My aim is for others to dump their screens for a few glorious hours and enjoy the healing, calming, fascinating world of home-grown gardens.

5

PLANTING AND COMPANION PLANTS

What is a weed? A plant whose virtues have not yet been discovered.

— RALPH WALDO EMERSON

People may not all be equally sociable, but we all need social interaction to be happy. Some people are extreme extroverts and depend on others to get energized while others are highly introverted and find spending time with people far less pleasing, but they still do it because we need social interaction. Introverts are often more stuck on their terms when it comes to social interaction. They may prefer to only be surrounded by small crowds or even only prefer certain types of people. Regardless of where you are on this scale, running from one extreme type of personality towards the other, having access to social interaction on our terms makes us happy.

Why do I share this short discussion of the human psyche? Simply because plants are not that much different from people. Like us, plants prefer to be surrounded by other plants. Some plants are very picky over what plants they want as their neighbors while others are more relaxed about it. Then there are those plants that simply cannot stand each other and planting them next to each other will only strain them but also reduce their yield. The complete opposite is also true, as some types of plants encourage others to flourish.

In gardening, we refer to this phenomenon as companion planting. The more accurate manner to explain companion gardening in gardening terms would be to say that plants affect each other. This effect can be positive or negative and by familiarizing yourself with the effects plants have on each other, you can use it to your benefit and provide your plants with an optimal environment to grow in.

LOOKING BACK ON COMPANION PLANTING

Companion planting has been around in the gardening world for many years as people used to think that certain plants are friends and others are foes. In some areas, this way of planting is also known as intercropping, which is a planting method commonly used in China. We have come to learn that this is not just a gardening myth, and there are sufficient scientific findings that plants do affect each other (Pleasant, 2021b).

In contrast to the outdated way of thinking about companion plants I mentioned above, science shows us that there are far more friendly relationships between different plants than antagonizing ones. These findings are convincing and we now know that vegetables especially need to have other plants growing near them to flourish optimally (Pleasant, 2021b).

Companion planting relationships do not only exist between different types of vegetables, but flowers can also be great companions to vegetables and the other way around. Therefore, it will not hurt to include some flowers in your vegetable beds, as the right types of flowers can improve your yield.

There is plenty of widely available research regarding companion planting. Therefore, I suggest you rely on quality resources backed by scientific findings when you are ready to explore companion planting in your garden.

BENEFITS OF COMPANION GARDENING

There are several ways in which plants impact other plants in their proximity.

Attracting Pollinators

Plants need to attract enough pollinators to yield the crops you expect. However, not all plants attract pollinators equally well. So, including plants that do attract a lot of pollinators to your garden, will entice them to visit the surrounding plants, ensuring proper pollination of all your plants, and helping them to produce the crops you are hoping to harvest.

Absorbing Certain Elements

There may be elements present in your garden soil that do not sit well with some of your plants. You can overcome this challenge by growing plants in the same area that absorb high levels of these elements, and so improve the soil quality for those plants that do not do well with exposure to the specific element. A good (but extreme) example of this is using sunflowers to rid the soil of radioactive contaminants in Fukushima, Japan.

Keeping Pests at Bay

Plants contain natural chemicals that can either attract or repel certain pests and even prevent diseases. So, the chemicals in one plant can repel the pests that usually attack another and if you grow these plants close to each other, one will keep the other safe.

Improving Nitrogen Levels

When we discussed soil health, we touched on the importance of nitrogen and how it is one of the elements in the soil that escapes relatively easily. Therefore, when you have plants that add nitrogen to the soil, like legumes, they will increase the nitrogen levels, benefitting all plants in that area.

Providing Shade

Some plants tend to grow a little taller than others, providing shade to those growing at a lower height. This shade serves as protection for plants that do not do well in full sun improving the overall environment for all plants in your garden.

Offering Support

Some plants are woodier and can stand tall even when they are in the wind, while others are flimsier and more vulnerable to structural damage. The latter group may also find it hard to stay upright without support but they can get support from being near sturdier plants. So, by planting these two types of plants near each other, you can protect more vulnerable plants.

Improving Soil Health

Plants do not only absorb nutrients from the soil they also add to the soil, even if it is only by changing the soil structure. The benefits one plant brings to the soil can be exactly what another needs from the soil to improve its growth.

Fewer Weeds

When you have entire beds planted with crops that grow tall and offer little ground cover, you are far more likely to find a lot of weeds, as there are larger pieces of open soil for the weeds to grow. But if you grow plants that do offer a lot of ground cover between these tall growing plants, they will reduce the number of weeds that will end up in your soil. It is an effective way to cut back on the time you would spend weeding your garden.

COMPANION PLANTING RELATIONSHIPS

Are you ready to see what plant combinations work well and how they benefit each other? Here is a selection of plants you can include in your vegetable garden, using the natural features of plants in your favor—you will notice several flowering plants in the list too.

Basil

Photo by Magda Ehlers

This herb is commonly found in herb gardens across the globe. The best companions for basil are tomatoes, peppers, and purslane. A quick side note on purslane which is often a widely underrated addition to the garden. Purslane is often considered to be a weed that needs to be ripped from the ground, but it is, in fact, edible and sometimes referred to as a vegetable. Its leaves are fat as the plant has an almost succulent-like appearance and is loaded with nutrients. Purslane is a wonderful ground cover, but it can also be eaten raw or cooked (Palsdottir, 2017). When planted together with basil, purslane can act as a ground cover protecting the soil around the basil from heat. The relationship becomes even more complex as in turn, the basil increases the flavor of the tomatoes and peppers growing nearby.

Cabbage

Consider adding sage and garlic to your cabbage patch, but do not dismiss planting nasturtiums either. The garlic will keep the cabbage safe from various pests while the sage does especially well in repelling cabbage moths. Nasturtiums are a beautiful bright and yellow addition to your garden, and you can add their flowers to salads to add a rich and peppery taste to the meal.

Furthermore, the nasturtiums will also deter aphids and beetles from visiting your cabbage.

Carrots

Carrots go well with quite a range of other plants, including leeks, sage, radishes, rosemary, peas, onions, and chives. When you have these all planted together, the chives will keep the carrots safe from mites, flies, and aphids. It also improves the growth curve and flavor of carrots. Rosemary and sage are two highly fragrant herbs that deter carrot flies while leeks protect your carrot crops from a range of pests.

Beets

Beets do great when planted close to bush beans, lettuce, onions, and garlic. Beets tend to increase the mineral content of the soil, improving the environment for their companions while onions keep the beets safe from cutworms and borers. Beets also go well with endive and chicory.

Lettuce

Lettuce can be easy to grow, but is quite vulnerable and often the target of many garden pests. Planting lettuce close to chives, onions, radishes, peas, oregano, or scallions will keep your lettuce harvest secure. It might seem like pests prefer lettuce because the leaves or soft and easy to eat, but it is, in fact, the scent of the lettuce that attracts pests. The scent of chives, garlic, and onion do a great job of hiding the lettuce scent from bugs while the basil adds flavor to the leaves. Sometimes the help offered takes on an even different form. By planting poached egg plants near your lettuce, you attract more hoverflies to your garden. Hoverflies love these wildflowers and they pose no risk to your lettuce, but they do eat the aphids that will attack your leafy greens.

Potatoes

Potatoes have lots of friends in the garden and you can add any or all of the following to your potato bed: basil, beans, horseradish, peas, tansy, garlic, cilantro, calendula, and oregano. Beans help to increase the size of your potatoes and cilantro is highly effective in keeping your crop protected from mites, aphids, spider mites, and beetles. Colorado potato beetles can cause havoc in a potato bed, but if you have calendula, horseradish, and tansy in the vicinity, these beetles will leave your garden alone. Another option here is catmint but be warned that catmint may also attract cats to your garden.

Spinach

Spinach grows relatively easily and even the most inexperienced gardener will be able to get a reasonable spinach harvest. There is one thing to which spinach is vulnerable and that is too much sunlight. Lengthy exposure to harsh sunlight will burn the spinach leaves. To prevent this, plant peas and beans in your spinach patch. Both these legumes are fast growers and as the plants can grow quite tall, they offer perfect shading to your spinach plants. Other friendly neighbors are strawberries, eggplant, cilantro, rosemary, and oregano. The last three on the list help to keep insects away.

Peppers

Basil, marjoram, onions, and oregano all protect your peppers from insects, while the basil will also increase the peppers' flavor.

Cucumbers

Tansy is another excellent flower to grow, so let us have a quick look at this herbaceous plant. Tansy can be invasive, so growing it is restricted in some areas and you would need to check whether this is the case in your region before planting it, but the plant adds a brilliant, beautiful color to your garden and it deters a wide range of bugs like ants, flying insects, and beetles. It also increases the flavor of cucumbers. Along with tansy, dill, lettuce, radishes, oregano, and nasturtiums go well with cucumbers. Dill steps up to protect cucumbers from aphids and mites. The strong aroma of oregano keeps insects at bay in general and the nasturtiums support growth and flavor but also serve to keep beetles and bugs at bay.

Tomatoes

Nematodes are attracted by tomatoes and can ruin the crops, but by planting asparagus close by, you can protect your harvest from these pests. The scent of basil deters a range of flying insects and spiders too, while it adds flavor to the tomatoes. The herb also attracts pollinators. Thyme deters armyworms from lying their eggs while dill does the same for cutworms. Calendula is another great partner as it helps to protect crops from a wide range of garden pests. Garlic, onion, and parsley also grow well when planted near tomatoes.

Peas

Do you add mint to your peas in the kitchen? Mint compliments the taste of peas wonderfully and by planting mint near your peas, you will improve the flavor while the peas are still in the pod. Chives keep the aphids away while peas also go well with carrots, lettuce, grapes, spinach, turnips, corn, radishes, and alyssum. The latter attracts pollinators to the garden as well as the predators feasting on aphids.

Zucchini

Consider planting buckwheat between your zucchini plants. Yes, buckwheat is a grain, but it also helps to attract predators to the garden that will eat the pests that attack zucchini. Other great neighbors for zucchini are oregano, zinnia, and nasturtium. While the nasturtium will keep the whiteflies and aphids under control, the oregano and zinnia attract pollinators.

Corn

Eating corn on the cob harvested straight from your own garden is surely one of the great pleasures for any gardener. Dill will keep your corn protected from aphids and mites. But there is another threat to your corn and that is wind. You can protect your corn from the force of strong gusts by planting sunflowers or even dwarf sunflowers in between. Beans will increase the nitrogen level in the soil to provide for the corn's needs and while your corn is doing well, plant spinach in between as the corn offers plenty of shade for the spinach to flourish in.

DIFFERENT WAYS TO COMPANION PLANT

While it is all good to know what plants work well with others and how they do it, you might still be stuck on the question of what technique to follow. The simplest way to bring in companion planting is through a monoculture garden. This means that you use one raised garden bed and plant different plants in between each other. You can plant a row of one plant, followed by a row of another.

Another option is to plant, for example, garlic in a circle, and then plant spinach in the center of the garlic. When plants are also good ground covers, you can plant them or sow their seeds in the same spot without any defined pattern. Like when you would plant strawberries between your watermelons.

An example we can borrow from Chinese gardeners and their intercropped gardens is to sow the seeds of one vegetable followed by that of another. A great example here would be to first sow kale and then follow it up with radishes, and once that is done, sow your tomatoes and celery. Sometimes these plants do not even have to be right on top of each other, as tomatoes and basil can be planted a foot apart from each other to enjoy the mutual benefits they offer to each other.

INCOMPATIBLE PLANTS

Have you ever had a neighbor who simply worked on your nerves? Maybe they are too noisy for your liking or their trees are constantly shedding leaves in your yard. It can be a pain to live in close proximity to someone who you are just not compatible with. In most cases, people can still get by without liking their neighbors but disliking someone can take an entirely different level of discomfort if you live in the same house. It may have started out with one thing they did that upset you but then all the little things that did not even upset you that much before start to spin out of control and soon everything they do annoys you, right?

Plants are the same. Certain plants should not be planted near each other as they do not do well in such situations. While the number of incompatible plants is far lower than the ones that are compatible, it is important to familiarize yourself with these plant combinations. If you do not avoid planting them close to each other, you are actively slowing down the progress you hope to see in your garden.

Some plants need lots of water and tend to pinch this vital water supply from their neighbors. The same is true with nutrients as some plants have higher nutrient demands and they will steal what they need to survive from the other plants around them. One way to prevent this nastiness in your garden is to keep a distance between plants that do not do well next to each other, and to provide sufficient space for individual fertilizing and watering.

Allelopathic plants take this unfriendly neighborly relationship to an even worse level for they tend to steal resources and their root systems invade those of plants nearby. The plants best known for showing such behavior are weeds, but it is not only limited to weeds. Scientific findings indicate that even the roots of some crops can leave chemicals in the soil after being uprooted, which will penetrate the roots of any surrounding plants (Waterworth, 2021).

While the field of allelopathic behavior in the garden still requires a lot of research, the following crops have been identified as having these features:

- cucumbers
- beets
- asparagus
- cabbage
- tomatoes
- broccoli

Fortunately, it seems that once these plants have been harvested and removed from the soil, the allelopathic elements only remain present in the soil for 10 to a maximum of 25 days.

Other plant combinations to avoid include cabbage and strawberries while planting cabbage, corn, dill, potatoes, or cauliflower near tomatoes will also reduce your tomato harvest and even strain the plant's growth. You should also protect your potato hills from cucumbers, radishes, squash, tomatoes, and sunflowers.

However, in the veggie garden, the list of companion plants is much longer than the one of plants that have poor neighborly relations.

Understanding how various plants can support each other and also which plants you should not plant too close to each other will help you with planning your garden. If you are a first-time gardener, make sure to do proper research before planting whatever you feel like. As a gardener, you will enjoy a lot of freedom, but it will also be to your benefit to know the features of each plant you are adding to your garden to be able to use its natural features in your favor. So, rather than seeing these guidelines as gardening restrictions, determine how you can maximize the natural properties of your plants.

By keeping a gardening journal, you will also be able to see how you can improve your ability to use companion planting to your benefit. Record the size and details of your yield and capture images and records of the order in which you plant different vegetables to see what worked and what needs attention.

It is now time to shift our focus to what you should add on top of your garden to keep the soil—and plants—in great shape throughout the planting season.

6

MULCHING AND WATERING

An unmulched garden looks to me like some naked thing which for one reason or another would be better off with a few clothes on.

— RUTH STOUT

Before going deeper into why mulching is such an important step in proper garden maintenance, I want to clarify what mulching is and explore the different forms it can take.

WHAT IS MULCH?

Mulch is a layer that you add onto the surface of your raised garden beds. Its primary purpose is to protect the soil, but depending on what kind of mulch you use, it can also have other roles to fulfill. While there are several kinds of mulch you can use, they all fall into one of two categories: organic mulch and inorganic mulch.

Inorganic mulch is not so common in smaller home gardens and is mostly something you will see on large commercial farms. Yet, if you feel that this solution that will better suit your garden, then feel free to use it.

Inorganic Mulch

Inorganic mulch can be subdivided into plastic fabrics and stones or gravel to use on top of garden beds.

Plastic Fabric

There are pros and cons when you use this material in your garden beds. You may find that plastic is an easier way to cover your garden beds or that it is less messy to work with and even though it may not look great, you can always cover it with a ground cover like pieces of bark.

This plastic tends to heat up quite a bit during the warmer seasons and due to this heat, it kills all the weeds that may be present. But it also kills the seeds of everything else that is not weeds. The easiest way to lay plastic sheets is to cover your entire bed before planting and to secure the plastic in its position. Then you can make holes in the plastic sheets and plant young seedlings in the holes. Plastic fabric can be used in beds you are not planning to work on during the year and where the plants do not require any fertilizer during their growing season. This is why you will often see that strawberry farmers choose plastic fabric to cover their beds.

The greatest disadvantage of plastic fabric as a ground cover is that plastic disintegrates over time. While plastic may take a very long time to break down in nature, it does not do well with persistent exposure to the elements. Once the plastic starts to disintegrate, it will most definitely release the chemicals present in the plastic into your soil. So, you need to ask yourself if this is something you want to happen.

If not, rather consider using gravel.

Gravel and Stones

Gravel and stones also build up a lot of heat in the warmer seasons which it releases into the soil, creating the same heating effect as plastic. As these stones or gravel can get quite hot, it is better to use it only in beds where you will be planting hardier plants. One more con to this kind of inorganic mulch is that if you change your mind, picking up all the stones and clearing your raised bed can be quite a pain.

Organic Mulch

You can consider all the types of mulch falling into this category as my favorites to use.

Bark

You can use bark in beds that need little work to sustain an optimal environment for plants. Bark will take by far the longest to disintegrate of all the other organic mulch in this category, making it a wonderful option to add to the pathways in your garden. While one benefit of bark is that it disintegrates slowly, it is also a disadvantage you will have to consider before using it as mulch. Since bark takes so long to disintegrate, you will find that by the next planting season the bark will still be almost completely intact in your beds. When you need to work on your garden beds and prepare them for the next season, it will require that you either try to work around the bark or remove as much of it as possible—which is never everything. Would planting around pieces of bark that might have ended up inside your beds be a problem for you? If not, feel free to use bark, otherwise, I suggest that you continue reading first.

Leaves

Dry leaves can end up in your garden without any effort on your part. Trees naturally shed their leaves in the autumn and will take some of the hard work away from you providing a free delivery of mulch. Soil that is covered with leaves tends to contain more and healthier earthworms. These leaves blend in quickly and as they also form a protective mat, this kind of mulch repels water on rainy days.

Pine Needles

The most prominent feature of pine needles is that they change the pH level in soil and make it more acidic. If this is something you are looking for, using pine needles will make perfect sense, but if you are already working on bringing the soil in your beds up to a higher level of alkalinity, then it is best to opt for something else. Pine needles work well to keep weeds out of the garden and keep your raised beds moist for longer. An excellent choice for blueberry beds.

Grass Cuttings

Cut grass is highly effective in preventing weeds from showing their tiny heads in your raised garden beds. It retains moisture as well but remember that grass is high in moisture content and it will break down much faster than any dry organic material. When it does break down, it can turn into a green, slimy, smelly mess. If you have used pesticides or any other chemicals on your lawn, it is best to discard the grass cuttings as these will release the chemicals into your soil.

When you have a lot of grass cuttings, you can also choose not to use it as mulch and simply add it to your composting heaps or bins to break down first before adding it to your soil as a form of nutrients.

Coconut Husk

Coconut husk, also known as coir, can serve as a wonderful mulch. It too prevents weeds from taking over in your raised beds and as it decomposes relatively quickly, it releases chemicals into the soil, adding to its richness. Furthermore, it can make your beds look really attractive.

Straw and Hay

These two types of mulch are by far the go-to choices for most vegetable gardens, regardless of whether they have raised garden beds or not. As these are cheap options that decompose quickly and in the process release nutrients into the soil and also keep soil-borne disease away from your plants, it is easy to understand why so many gardeners choose straw or hay as mulch. Once the growing season is over, you can easily work the leftover straw or hay into the soil and it helps to prepare the soil for the next planting season.

The options I have mentioned are not the only types of mulch you can choose from as the list also includes nut shells, peach pits, and more. See what types of organic mulch you can acquire cheaply or that require a minimal time investment.

WHEN TO MULCH?

When is the best time to add mulch to your garden beds? This will largely depend on your climate. If you face severely cold winters, consider adding mulch in the fall. By adding a thick layer of soil and even manure, you can create a layer that will protect the soil during the winter and release nutrients into your garden.

The other preferred time to mulch is in spring. When the weather starts warming up and the soil is busy drying out for summer, a layer of mulch will benefit your new garden greatly. However, if spring in your region is still too much of a wet season, it is better to wait a bit until it is closer to summer and the soil is a bit drier. The average regional temperatures will also play a role. In warmer regions, it is better to add a thicker layer of mulch while a thin layer will give you better results in a cooler area.

WHY SHOULD YOU MULCH?

Now that you are familiar with the basics regarding mulching, it is time to grasp the many benefits of this season's garden activity. There are many good reasons why you should not skip adding mulch to your garden.

Mulch Enriches the Soil

As organic mulch gradually breaks down, it slowly releases all the nutrients it contains into the soil. This replaces the nutrients lost from the soil through plant uptake and exposure to the natural elements. The mulch layer also slows down the process of nutrients leaching out of the soil in your garden beds.

It Offers Several Types of Protection

Do you want to save money by taking sufficient preventative measures to avoid having to deal with pests and diseases? Mulch is the answer. It is the one thing that can single-handedly serve as your garden's immune system, keeping disease, pests, and weeds to the minimum. It also offers protection to young seedlings, shielding them from the wind and offering a little more shade to plants during this tender stage. Another form of protection you can expect from mulch is reduced soil erosion, as your garden beds will lose less soil through water running off the surface. Whether it is rain or water from your watering hose, water droplets beat down on loose soil, compacting it to a certain degree but also washing away the soil particles. After several rounds of watering, you will find plant roots can become exposed, and even seedlings can be washed away completely. Not to mention the loss of nutrients your garden beds will experience. Mulch breaks up the water before it hits the soil keeping it intact.

Mulch Saves Water

Having a water-wise garden can be extremely beneficial, especially in drier regions where water can be scarce. Vegetable gardens, however, need a lot of water, but by adding mulch on top of your garden beds, you will have to water it less often. The mulch serves as a shield to prevent evaporation and far less water will get lost by simply running off the surface of your garden beds during watering or rain. Not only will you save money on water, but also on time as you will be watering your garden less often.

It Regulates Soil Temperature

In areas with adverse weather conditions and severe temperature shifts, garden soil can easily take a punch from nature. Mulch provides a wonderful barrier to keep soil warmer during the very cold seasons while ensuring that all that is underneath it remains cooler during the hottest season.

Mulch Supports Life in Soil

Mulch adds nutrients to the soil but also improves the biological activity you want to have in your garden. The layer of organic material becomes home to many microorganisms that help the matter to decompose. This decomposed material also improves the soil structure, keeps the soil from compacting, and creates a more favorable environment for plant roots to grow and sustain life on a micro level.

It Looks Pretty

A layer of mulch also creates a clean surface for your crops to fall on when they are ripe without having any contact with the soil. Mulch makes your garden beds look finished off nicely and it improves the visual appeal these offer to your garden.

A FEW MULCHING TIPS

Mulching your garden is really as easy as adding a layer on top of the soil. When you add organic mulch, make sure that you add a thick layer so that your garden beds can enjoy all the benefits I have expanded on. What would be a thick layer? Aim to add a layer that is about eight inches thick. I know it sounds like a lot of mulch, but remember that this layer compacts over time, and if it is not thick enough, it will become an added dried-out layer on top of your beds that can be messy and utterly useless. This layer gets the most sun and wind exposure and by making sure that it is thick, you can overcome this challenge. Compost is rich in nutrients and you want all of that goodness to go into your soil, but if you add compost on top, it will lose its potent richness and all its benefits will be wasted. So, add compost to your soil, but always add a thick layer of mulch on top. Mulch is cheap enough—and often available for free—so do not skimp on it.

WATERING

So, we know that watering plants regularly is important and that it is vital to ensure that soil remains moist. We also know that the soil on the edges of these beds tends to dry out the quickest. What I want to expand on now are the different options you have to water your raised beds.

Sure, you can use a watering hose or a watering can. You can also use an irrigation system as mentioned earlier, but there is more. I am not going to expand on how to use a watering hose—I am sure you know how to—but I want to emphasize that you should always use a hose with care. Always be aware of where your watering hose is lying, making sure it is not resting on any plants. If you are not careful while using a watering hose, it can become one of the most destructive things to bring into your garden. When filled with water, a hose can become surprisingly heavy and if you are going to pull it through your raised beds, it is bound to bend some delicate plant stems off or tear some leaves. Therefore, always make sure that you have a hose that is long enough to reach even the parts of your garden furthest away from the tap. Plan your watering routine in such a manner that you know at all times where your hose should go, and always use low pressure. If your hose fitting offers different settings, use the one that is the closest to a fine mist as the smaller the droplets are the less impact they have on the soil and your plants. You may have added mulch to reduce water run-off and soil erosion, but by using low pressure to water your garden, you can prevent such risks even better.

The latter is also true when you use a watering can. These can be heavy to hold above your bedding and it may be tempting to get as much water out as quickly as possible. By doing this, you are likely going to wash open the plant roots or uproot fragile seedlings completely. Always use a head on your can that gives out a gentle trickle to give the soil the moisture it needs without causing any damage or harm to your garden.

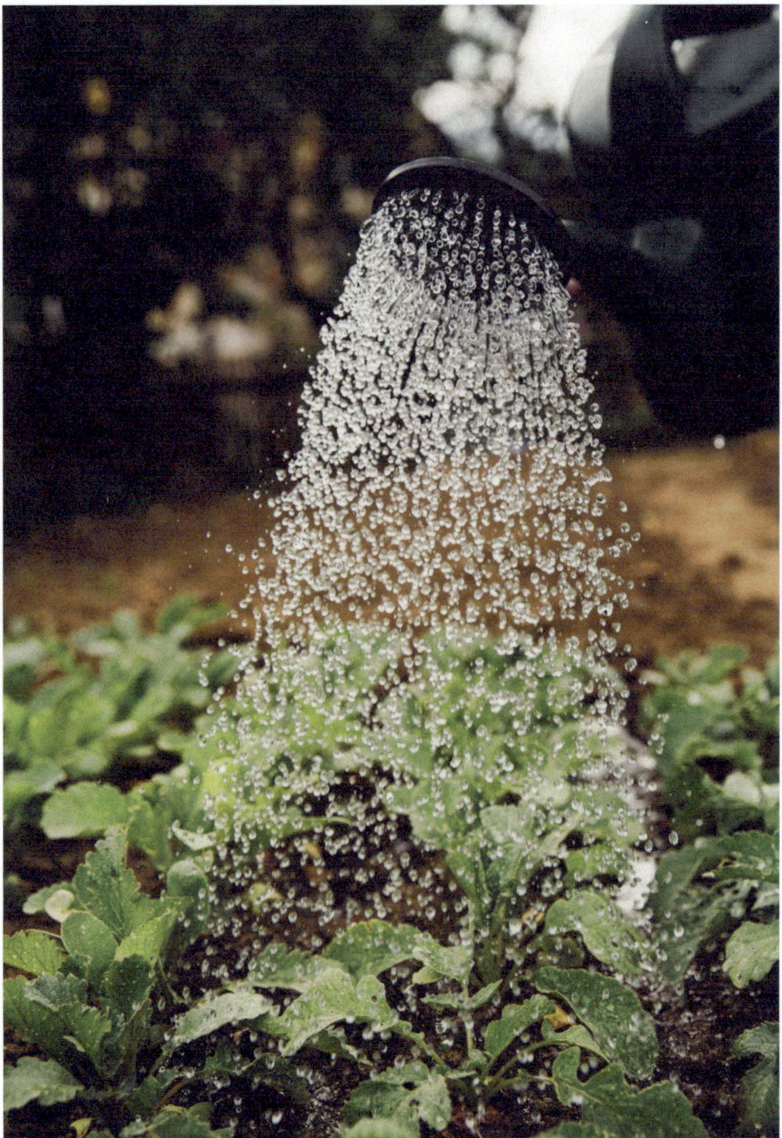

ALTERNATIVE WATERING SOLUTIONS

The following are all unconventional but highly effective ways to water raised garden beds. Some of these solutions rely on recycled material and can even be described as simply genius.

Water Jug Irrigation

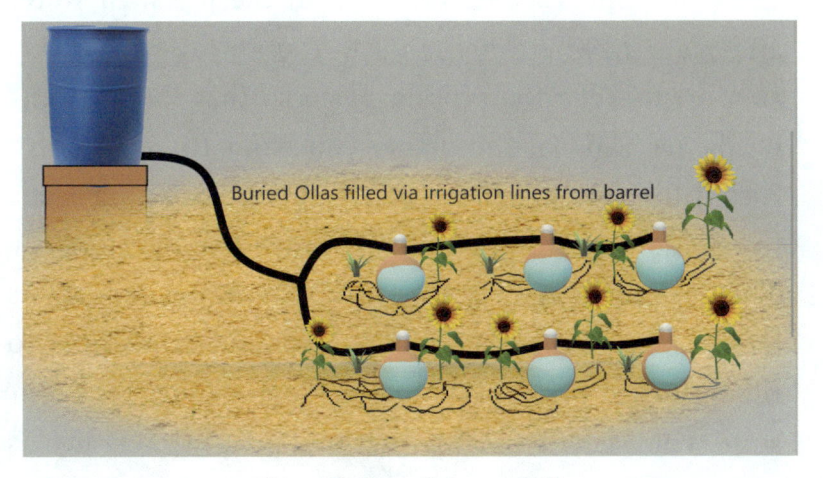

Copyright James Roberson 2023

For this, you will need a recycled plastic container, different containers will give you different solutions. One impressive option is to use a water dispenser refill can and a piece of black irrigation pipe that is as long as your raised bed is wide. Drill two holes big enough for a piece of black plastic pipe to fit through them in a straight line. You can drill these holes about an inch from the bottom making sure that the two holes are perfectly aligned. Push the piece of pipe through the two holes and seal it off with glue or silicon. Take your design to your garden and place the empty can where it would be a great fit and then insert drip irrigation nozzles in the black pipe. Place stoppers at both ends of the pipe to seal it off.

Once all your sealants are dry, fill the jug with water and place it where it fits best. You can use irrigation support to keep the pipe in place so that the dripping heads are right at the plants you want to keep moist. After filling the jug with water, open the dripping heads to release just a few droplets of water onto your plants. This dripping system is bound to keep your plants moist and will save you a lot of effort. You only need to fill up the jug once it is empty and can be sure that your soil will remain moist without disturbing it. As pictured above you can use this method to fill ollas which further reduces your watering schedule.

Wicking Beds

What is a wicking bed exactly? Wicking beds offer an effective solution to keep the soil moist and as the water is at the bottom of the bed and not being irrigated from the top, there is far less evaporation, making this the preferred choice in countries where water is scarce. Essentially, the water gets drawn upwards toward the plant instead of draining down to the bottom of the container. It is a solution you can easily create at home, but you will have to decide on this watering solution in advance as it will require that you do all your planting and build your raised bed inside the container that serves as the wicking bed. You can make your wicking bed from recycled material as you will need a large watertight container and a couple of pipes, sand, gravel, and soil, but it should not take more than half a day's work to install your self-watering garden.

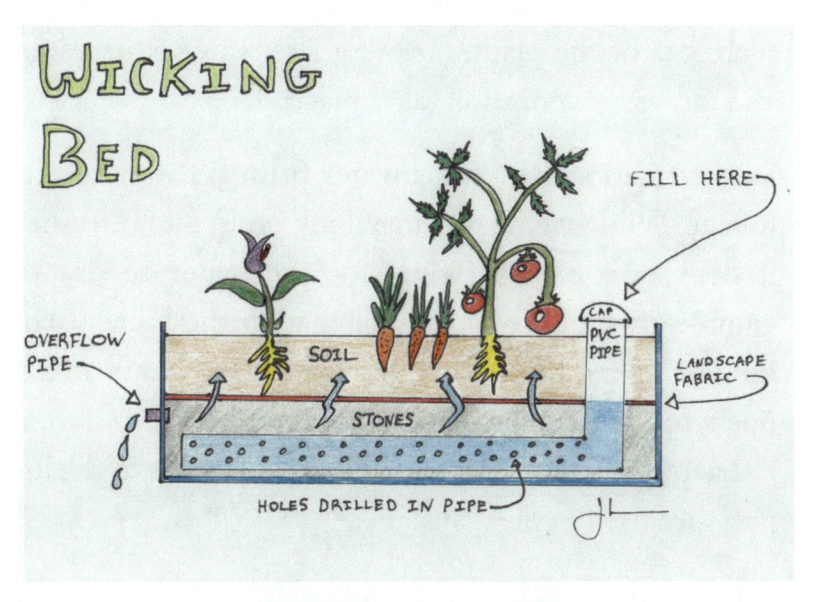

Copyright James Roberson 2023

Drip Irrigation

The best time to consider what kind of watering system you are going to use is when you are still planning your garden. However, even if you have decided against it at first, and are convinced later on that drip irrigation is the way to go, you will still be able to bring this watering solution to your garden with minimal effort.

It is often only after you have experienced the struggles of controlling a water hose enough times that you may realize the benefits to drip irrigation. Benefits such as reduced water usage, as the water is directed only to the roots of the plant, meaning less water is necessary and far less evaporation takes place.

Drip irrigation also keeps water from getting onto the foliage. While wet leaves may look clean and refreshed, it does take a bit of time for the water to dry off completely and this causes damage to the foliage. This kind of irrigation will never wash away your soil or open up the roots of your plants. So, the runoff of nutrient-rich soil is far less, which is also due to the low pressure used in these systems.

While drip irrigation is a wonderful way to keep the soil moist, it is not a solution that is entirely problem-free. At times you would need to clear up the holes as they are so tiny, they can get clogged. There is also an initial expense linked to such an installation and it does require regular maintenance. But still, it is by far the most effective and beneficial form of irrigation you can use in your raised garden beds.

Ollas

Courtesy of Dripping Springs Ollas

Ollas are an ancient irrigation method that you have quite likely never heard of before. It is an entirely passive way of keeping the soil in your garden beds moist. But how does it work? Ollas are unglazed clay pots buried underneath the soil and as the clay allows water to seep out into the soil, it keeps the soil surrounding the pot moist. The key here is to use unglazed pots. Glazed clay pots are completely watertight and the water will not be able to penetrate through the pot and into the soil. The pot also needs to have a narrow neck, as this shape limits the amount of water lost through evaporation.

Courtesy of Dripping Springs Ollas

When you *plant* an olla, it is important to keep the neck of the pot above the surface while the round part at the bottom is completely covered by the soil. As the soil around the pot loses moisture, it will naturally draw moisture from the inside of the pot, through the clay surface. This is a method that works so well, that the roots of the plants around these pots actually start to grow toward the ollas to suck up the water it needs.

If this is the kind of watering system you would like to use in your garden, then it would be best to install your ollas first and then sow the seeds or plant seedlings afterward. As these fragile plants will need sufficient water, but can easily be disturbed through conventional watering methods, an olla is a perfect way to ensure enough moisture in the soil without any wastage. In fact, ollas can reduce your water consumption anywhere between 50 to 70% while still providing the soil with all the moisture it needs (Epic Gardening, 2022). As you will be filling your ollas manually, you can easily use gray water to save even more water. I would definitely recommend this way of irrigation for gardens in dry areas. I have found that the Dripping Springs Ollas (dsollas.com)seem to be the most ideal.

Now you are left with one question—how big an area do the ollas cover? The size of the olla's diameter determines the diameter that the water will spread, but essentially, you will have to plant within 2-3 feet the ollas because if your plants are planted too far away from the pots, the water will simply not reach the roots.

Even though ollas are a preferred method to use in dry areas, it does not mean you cannot use them in colder regions too. However, if this is the case, you will have to dig them up and remove them from the soil to protect the pots from ground freezing as cold temperatures can cause them to crack and you will have lost your pot. While ollas are specifically designed for this purpose, you can also use any other shaped unglazed terracotta pots. Simply seal the hole at the bottom, bury them and fill them with water, and place the clay tray on to form a lid. That said, I personally find that the ollas work much better.

So, there you have it. The more you get into gardening the more you will be inspired to experiment with different solutions to bring you the results you seek. I recommend that you start with the basics to help build your knowledge and experience in the garden, but that you gradually expand your knowledge to include various methods of planting, mulching, and watering and even use some of these established methods to find solutions that address your garden's unique challenges. Next up we will take a look at fencing and how to protect your garden against all kinds of threats.

7

FENCING/PLANTING FLOWERS TO KEEP PESTS AWAY

The final principle of natural farming is no pesticides. Nature is in perfect balance when left alone.

— MASANOBU FUKUOKA

One of the many beautiful and often encouraging reasons why people begin to explore gardening is because of the complete control they have over what crops they harvest. Raised garden beds offer a safe way to consume fresh vegetables without exposure to pesticides. That said, the ambition to be naturally green and healthy can be under attack in your raised garden. The force trying to shift your mind in a different direction and lead you into the temptation to get out the pesticide can and spray your beautiful crops with all kinds of chemicals has natural origins. Yes, it is often bugs and other natural pests posing a threat to your crops. At times, the devastation these pesky little threats can cause takes the form of a gradual decline. But there are also moments when they can cause immense damage overnight.

How do you prevent it without adding any unwanted chemicals to your precious green space? There are many natural or organic options to choose from to protect your garden and keep it a green zone producing only healthy crops.

NATURAL WAYS TO ADDRESS GARDEN PESTS

Pests can come in all shapes and forms. You may have a problem with bugs, worms, moths, or other insects that will eat holes in leaves and nestle themselves deep inside the fruits of your labor.

Start From the Ground Up

The quality of your soil will to a large extent impact the number of pests you have to fight off in your garden. Your first line of defense is ensuring you have healthy soil. We have discussed soil in great detail already in chapter two, so there is not much left to say in this regard. However, I want to remind you that it is a good practice to have your soil tested annually if budget allows, to see the exact state of the foundation of your garden. These results will indicate what you need to add and in which areas your soil is performing perfectly fine.

Even when lab results indicate that your soil needs some additional care, refer back to chapter two to see how you can address these concerns organically. Why? Because chemical fertilizers and pesticides may appear like they can deliver the outcome you are hoping for, but they harm the natural organisms present in the soil. These microorganisms help to keep your soil healthy and they do their bit to keep pests at bay, so adding anything that does not favor them will leave your garden in a worse state. Rather keep it natural and bring your soil to the level it needs to be by relying on natural sources, supporting the life in your soil. Healthy soil supports healthy plants and healthy plants are much less at risk of being attacked by pests. As these plants are stronger, they also recover much faster from any damage caused by pests.

Regular Spring Cleaning

For the very same reasons you would keep your home clean, you should also keep your garden clean. You would not leave rotten fruit lying around in your kitchen, so you should not leave them lying in your garden either. When these fruits have fallen and are just left to rot, they become a place for bugs and pests to breed and this can cause an infestation in your garden. If these rotten plant parts are left for too long, it also provides the perfect environment for bugs to stay during the winter. Spring cleaning of your garden will also mean getting rid of all the infested parts of the garden. Do not add any plant parts that are damaged to your compost as it will affect your compost quality. Rather discard them where they will not have any contact with your garden.

Create a Sanctuary for Helpful Bugs

There are many bugs that you would want to have in your garden. This is not only because you need them for pollination, but also because a lot of pests will stay away when certain bugs are around. By creating an inviting space for garden-friendly bugs, you can be sure that at least some of the pests you want to keep away will be far less of a problem. You can transform your garden into a happy bug haven by ensuring that there are enough flowers to attract them and by providing shelters and space where they can find protection from their predators. The life you want to attract to your garden includes ladybugs, bees, praying mantes, hoverflies, dragonflies, salamanders, frogs, and even lizards. Before killing or removing any bugs, research them first to see if you should welcome the specific species rather than kill it.

A Garden Is a Lot Like a Relationship

The more time you invest in your relationships, the stronger and happier they will become. The same is true for your garden. The more time you spend in your garden, the healthier your plants will be. By being in your garden more often, you will be able to spot problems before they get out of hand. This is when you will notice pest eggs in your garden, especially under leaves, and should remove the entire leaf before the creepy crawlies take off into every corner. What should you do when you see any adult pests? Check for eggs underneath plant leaves in the vicinity. These grown-up pests will lay eggs in your garden as they see it as an inviting space to help sustain the next generation.

Rotate Crops

Even if you have found the perfect spot for your lettuce to grow and feel tempted to use the same spot over and over, do not repeat the same plant spacing, otherwise you are putting your garden at risk of an infestation.

Getting Rid of Pets Through Companion Planting

In chapter five, we discussed the many benefits of companion planting and one of the benefits that plants often offer to their neighbor plants is pest control. You can use the following plants to deter the most commonly found garden pests.

- **ants**: garlic, tansy, mint, spearmint, catmint, and pennyroyal all keep ants at bay.
- **aphids**: plant nasturtiums, basil, onions, stinging nettle, garlic, or spearmint to keep aphids from causing damage in your garden.
- **caterpillars**: garlic and tomato leaves repel caterpillars. You can also sprinkle black pepper on the leaves to keep them from ruining your crops.
- **slugs**: slugs do not like garlic
- **fruit flies**: basil and tansy are helpful aids
- **cabbage butterfly**: protect cabbage by planting rosemary, mint, dill, spearmint, tansy, thyme, sage, or garlic around the cabbage.
- **mildew**: plant mildew ruins your crops but you can prevent it by planting chives and nettle around the plants at risk of mildew.
- **fungus**: stinging nettle, horseradish, and sage prevent fungus

- **mice**: mice do not like spearmint and mint and the strong scent of wormwood also keeps them away.

Use Polyculture Planting

Monoculture is what you will typically see on commercial farms. Large fields of wheat, corn, potatoes, or anything else produced on a large scale. The disadvantage of this kind of planting is that if you have one plant that is affected by a pest, the problem quickly spreads to affect other plants. Commercial farms deal with these infestations by spraying crops with pesticides worth thousands of dollars. You most probably do not want to expose your garden to these chemicals or spend that much money on keeping your plant safe. This is where polyculture comes in. By planting a variety of plants—preferably companion plants—you prevent plants from being spotted by the pests that prefer them as they are hidden amongst other plants. The different scents in your garden offer a type of shield and keep plants from being found by the bugs that can harm them. So, just by mixing various kinds of plants in your garden, you can prevent infestations and keep your garden organic.

Grow Insect Repelling Plants

I have mentioned before that growing flowering plants in your raised vegetable garden beds can add visual appeal, but they can also improve the state of your garden. The predominant way flowers contribute to the health of a vegetable garden is through their scent which repels a range of pests.

The following flowers will bring beauty and security to your raised garden beds.

Hyssop

Hyssop grows in magnificent strings of purple-blue flowers and is a great companion to plant in your cabbage patch. One of the most common threats to cabbage is the cabbage moth, which is a pest that does not like the scent of hyssop flowers.

Borage

Borage thrives in gardens with cooler average temperatures and has a dainty blue bloom. Bees and other pollinators flock to these plants but it is also a wonderful repellent for tomato hornworms and cabbage worms.

Catmint

When catmint is in bloom, your beds are covered in a purple wave that not only keeps insects away but also causes deer and rabbits to rather go somewhere else for a meal. While it keeps these pests at bay, hummingbirds simply love them and you are bound to attract some of these feathered friends to your yard.

Calendula

Do you have rich, well-drained soil in full sunlight or even partial shade? Add these deep yellow almost orange flowers to your beds to keep your crops safe from nematodes, asparagus beetles, and tomato hornworms.

Copyright Kaznacheeva /Dreamstime

Lavender

Lavender is known for the magnificent purple spread it makes and its strong scent. While the plant is relied on in calming remedies, it is not a scent enjoyed by garden pests. If you have well-drained soil that enjoys full sunlight near your garden beds, fill the space with lavender. Just be wary of root rot as lavender may be hardy but is susceptible to diseases linked to excessive moisture.

Russian Sage

The plant makes blueish flowers that attract bees and other pollinators. However, as the plant has hardy branches and rather fuzzy foliage, other bugs show no interest. So, planting these around your garden will drastically reduce the number of pests you need to fight later on.

STEPS YOU CAN TAKE WHEN SPOTTING PESTS

There are several approaches you can follow once you have identified which pests you have in your garden. The severity of the action you need to take will depend on how severe the attack on your plants is. This can vary from only a few visible pests to a colony now calling your garden home.

Keep in mind though never to over-doctor your garden. Gardening requires patience. Sure, you will still have a garden when you jump right in with a sprayer and start to bomb all insects with whatever it is that is the most effective remedy—which can be an organic blend too—but rather avoid this. Always have a soft hand in your garden, even when it comes to pest control for you do not want to harm your garden and the life it contains by fighting off only one pest species. Remember that you are working with nature and nature is a very complex system where every action has some, even unforeseen, consequences. As this is the case, it may sometimes be better to just get rid of a plant entirely if it is heavily invested. The damage or infestation may be so severe that getting rid of the plant and the pests it contains may be the only effective—and least invasive—method to clear your garden.

You Can Do Nothing

This might not sound helpful at all, but always remember that your garden is part of nature and nature can take care of itself. Doing nothing is the approach I recommend if you know you are going to monitor the problem closely and have the time to inspect the affected plants daily. This way you will be able to see if the garden-friendly bugs are taking care of the pests or whether you need to step in. Plants are also not entirely helpless, especially if you have healthy plants growing in healthy soil. Most plants can recover from minor damage and still be perfectly fine.

Take Preventative Steps

When you have seedlings that are still very vulnerable to pests, you may want to provide an added shield that will keep them safe. Here, row covers can be a helpful aid and as the plant will still get sufficient sunlight and fresh air underneath these covers, you can be sure that it will recover and continue to grow strong until you can remove the covers when the plant is ready to tolerate damage.

Insect Traps

By attaching insect traps near plants that have been affected or are vulnerable to pests, you can get rid of a lot of unfriendly bugs. Make sure to use these discreetly as you are also going to trap some bugs that you would want in your garden. Another option is to set out organic traps. Something as simple as an orange cut in half and placed on the soil in affected areas will attract pests as they will see this as an enticing food source. Be sure to check these oranges daily, preferably first thing in the morning to see what you have caught in your traps. If you spot any friendly bugs that also came for a feast, you can always release them back into your garden.

There is also another way to catch pests, but it is only a solution for those less squeamish. Yes, you have guessed it: Certain pests are large enough that you can catch and remove them by hand. If you are scared that they will jump on you, schedule your hunting session for early in the morning as bugs move a little slower during this time of day.

Provide a Shield

Have you ever used garden collars? They are easy to make at home as you only need pieces of pipe with a large enough diameter to fit around young plants without restricting their growth. These collars create almost a fence around the young stems and reduce the number of pests that will attack your plants significantly.

Get Rid of Infested Plant Parts

Do not allow leaves or any other parts of plants that are infested in your garden. As pests gather on these leaves, you can simply cut back the leaves and by removing these parts, you are also removing a large part of your problem. Again—discard these plant parts away from the garden and make sure not to place them with your compost.

Wash Your Plants

Sometimes you can spray pests off the affected plant parts to solve the problem. The best time to do this is early in the morning as you would want the leaves to dry before the sunlight on them becomes too harsh. When there are droplets of water on plant leaves, they are more vulnerable to getting burned by the sunlight.

Organic Solutions

There are several organic solutions you can use to get rid of pests. My preferred option is garlic spray. You can spray this quite often and it does not cause any damage to your garden. The best feature of this spray is that it does not kill any pests but the smell does keep them away from your crops. While there are several other organic solutions you can use in your garden, these will always be my last resort as there are other natural ways to get rid of any concerns.

THE MOST COMMON GARDEN PESTS

Can you positively identify all the pests in your garden?

The following list contains the names of most of the pesky creatures you need to look out for.

- **Aphids** can be treated simply by spraying them with a hose or you can do nothing and see if nature takes care of them. If not, garlic spray will work.
- **Cabbage worms** can be stopped in their tracks by row covers, or you can remove them by hand. A more severe approach would be to use sticky traps.
- **Pill bugs** can be deterred by keeping your garden clean. If they do come into your garden, place a couple of citrus traps and clear them out early in the morning.
- **Cutworms** love to eat away at your crops underneath the surface. Garden collars pressed

down deep enough into the soil can prevent this from happening.
- **Flea beetles** will gather on the plant leaves so the best defense is to use row covers to keep your plants safe.
- **Leaf-footed bugs** are big enough to catch by hand. When you do, always check underneath surrounding plant leaves for their eggs.
- **Corn worms** can become food for other bugs, so be sure to attract these bugs to your garden. Garlic spray may also drive them away.
- **Whiteflies** gather on the surface of leaves and you can spray them off easily, but you can also use sticky traps to get rid of this pest.
- **Slugs** can cause severe damage, but you do not have to tolerate them in your garden. They are easy to remove by hand, or you can use row covers. By using crop rotation and keeping your garden clean, you will also minimize the chances of slugs in your garden.
- **Thrips** can be sorted out by spraying water on the plant or with garlic spray.
- **Spider mites** can easily be sprayed with water to get rid of them.
- **Tomato hornworms** are quite large, making it easy to remove them by hand. Row covers will

also keep your plants safe when you are not there to keep an eye on them.
- **Squash vine borers** eat holes into your crops. Crop rotation can prevent such an infestation and so will row covers. Otherwise, you can use garlic spray to get rid of them.

As important as it is to familiarize yourself with the pests that can move into your garden, you also need to get to know the different types of garden-friendly bugs that stay there. That way, you can keep the ones supporting your efforts safe.

THE IMPORTANCE OF FENCING

The pests that enter your garden and pose a risk to your crop yields are not always creepy crawlies. No, sometimes they can be fluffy and very cute to look at, but they can still cause a lot of damage. I am referring here to rodents like rabbits and mice and even larger threats like deer.

The perfect fence has a natural appeal while still offering plenty of protection. After all, you have created a beautiful natural space and you do not want it to look like it is imprisoned by the fence. Therefore, I am sharing some of my favorite fencing options, some of them being more affordable solutions than others.

The Hog Wire Fence

A hog wire fence has a wooden frame—hence the natural appeal—coupled with wire inserts offering outstanding protection for your garden.

ID 201479154 © Fiskness | Dreamstime.com

How you construct the fence will depend on the size and layout of your garden, but the ideal situation is to fence off a large enough area that offers protection to all your raised beds. You can use any kind of wooden poles that are tall enough to make a decent-height fence.

Start by measuring out the area you want to protect with your fence and mark it clearly on the soil. An easy way to do this is to use long nails with a string attached to them to provide secure lines of where the fence will go.

Next, you need to dig holes for the poles. Plant these poles no more than 9 ft apart. Attach wooden beams between these poles at the bottom of the fence and at the top. Now you will be able to attach the wire. Simply spread out your role of wire and attach them to the poles with a staple gun.

It is also important to consider the pest that can dig a hole underneath your fence. To offer protection in this regard, it is best to use plastic-covered mesh as you will be burying this part and you do not want it to corrode due to moisture exposure. First, dig out some of the soil on the outside of the fence deep enough to bury a protective layer of mesh. Cut strips of mesh, each about one and a half to two feet wide, and staple these onto the bottom wooden pole. Bury the loose side of the mesh stretched out underneath the soil. This will form a barrier keeping animals that like to dig their way into your garden, out. Remember to include a gate too for easy entry. To build a hog wire fence, you will need enough wooden poles and wire, a spade to dig holes for the poles, a drill or hammer, and screws or nails to attach the wire. A staple gun will also make the task much easier and do not forget the mesh you will need to provide protection underneath the surface.

As these materials are heavy to work with you may need to have assistance in erecting this fence. While a hog wire fence is not the most affordable fence option, it is also not the most expensive and it creates a perfectly decent-looking fence that can also serve as support for plants.

Wattle Fencing

In chapter four, I explained that wattle weaving is an affordable technique to make raised garden beds. This method may take a bit longer to complete but is made mostly of raw materials you can find in your surroundings—depending on where you stay. You can also use freshly pruned branches to make a wattle-weaving fence. The best wood to use for a wattle fence is the branches from prune, elder, apple, or ash trees. The process to construct such a fence is exactly the same as when you are using the technique to create a raised garden bed, now you will only be doing it on a larger scale.

Here too, you will have to measure and mark the area you want to protect. Then, you will have to plant stakes to create the foundation of your fence. These stakes need to be firmly set in the soil as you will be weaving the wattle branches around them. The stakes can be branches that you have pruned back on trees of a studier wood. You just need to clean them up and plant them deep enough to provide sufficient support for your fence.

Wattle fences are affordable to make and they can enhance the appearance of your garden, while also complementing your entire property. These fences also offer a secure barrier that will keep pesky animals out.

Your garden is now protected on both a micro level and on a much larger scale. We have indeed covered every aspect of what it entails to be a successful gardener. Even more important though is that I gave you all the tips and tricks you would need to make life as a gardener easy and enjoyable. After all, while the benefits of having a garden include having a constant supply of fresh vegetables and herbs, it should also be a task you love and you should enjoy the time you spend in your garden.

There is only one aspect that will impact your gardening success left to discuss and this is hardiness zones and how your location will impact your entire gardening venture.

8

PLANT PROFILES/PLANT HARDINESS CHARTS

Facts must be faced. Vegetables simply do not taste as good as most other things do.

— PEG BRACKEN

I find it interesting how easily people turn their opinions into facts simply by stating that it is the way it is. We can only hope that Peg Bracken meant it in a fun way as her readers are familiar with her sense of humor. However, the only truth in the above statement is that veggies bought from conventional retailers will never taste the same as the ones you harvest from your own garden. While the entire gardening process is an amazingly relaxing and rewarding experience, the epitome is surely when you walk your early morning rounds and can eat peas fresh from the pod, or when you draw radishes out of the soil and your hard work and diligence are rewarded with tasty juicy red and white bulbs. But before I get ahead of myself with a list of recommendations of what you can plant in your garden, we need to explore hardiness zones.

HARDINESS ZONES EXPLAINED

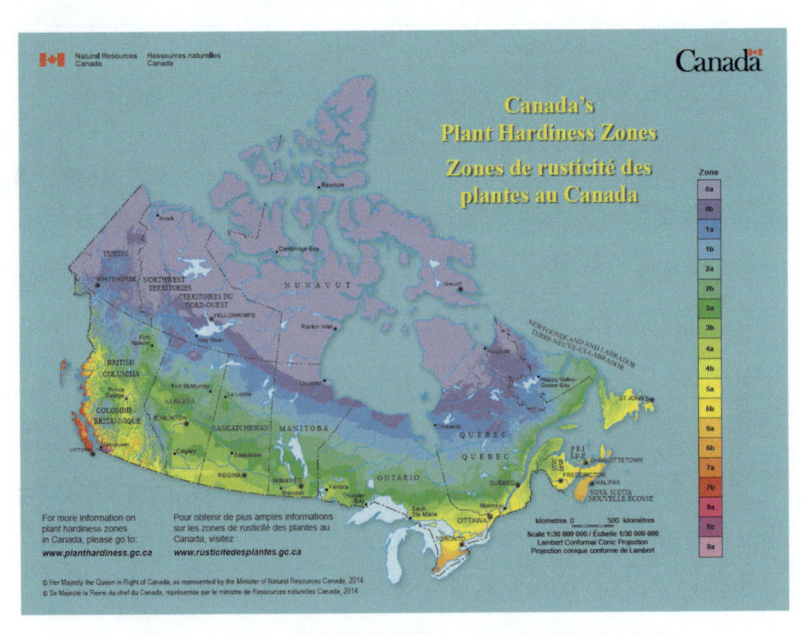

Courtesy of Natural Resources Canada

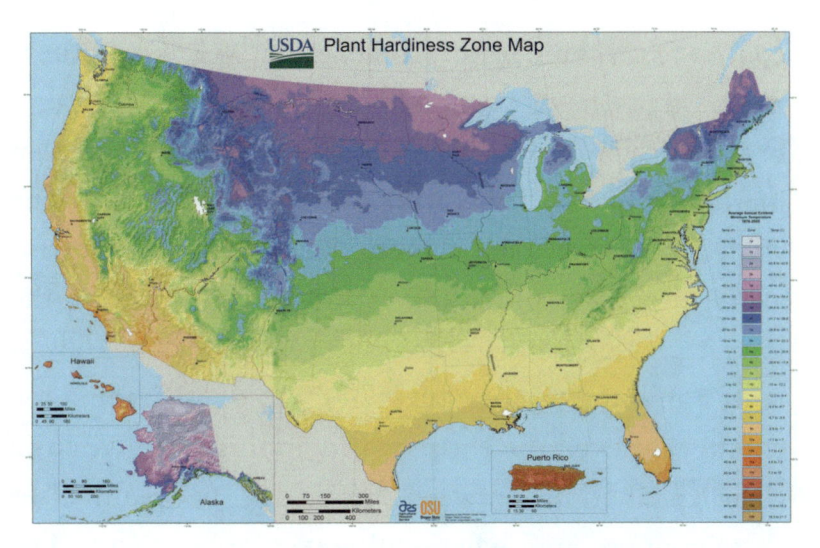

Courtesy of USDA Agricultural Research Service

Every single plant in your garden, surroundings, and even region is impacted by the hardiness zone of the area you are staying in. While every country in the world can be divided into different hardiness zones, I will only be focusing on these zones in the United States and Canada. Yet, regardless of what country you live in, the same determining factors for the different hardiness zones will apply to you too. Simply research the relevant government site to find your hardiness zone map.

To compile the hardiness zone map, climate data for every region is traced 30 years back to determine the average minimum temperatures for the region (Hassani, 2022). The map works on 10 zones and every zone counts for a temperature bracket of 10°F. Once these larger areas have been defined, each area is further broken down into an a and b area. These resemble an increment of 5°F. This rating starts at zone 1a, with the coldest region in the US being Alaska. Here the lowest average temperature is -60 to -55 °F. Compared to the lowest average temperature for a region such as Hawaii with minimum temperatures of 60 to 65°. Dividing the country, or even the entire world, in this way gives us a clear distinction between what can be planted in certain areas and what will never grow there. The hardiness zones also determine the length of the planting season, which is vital for gardeners to know.

So, how does the hardiness zone map impact your garden? Or, maybe a better question would be: What should you do to best manage your garden, including the times you plant and harvest to make the most of the planting season in your region? Before planting anything in your garden, whether it is seeds or seedlings, read the guidelines on the packaging. This will help you determine whether the specific plant will grow in your garden and when you should plant it. If this is still confusing, I recommend that you visit your local nursery as they mainly stock plants they know will grow in the specific hardiness zone.

An additional tip when it comes to hardiness zones is that the minimum temperature indicated for your region is the average minimum temperature, so it does not mean that it never gets any colder than that. You may experience times when it is way colder than what the map indicates, but this will not be the average temperature. How does this impact your gardening? If you are going to choose plants that are only suitable for your region and you do not have an exceptionally cold winter—meaning it does not get colder than the average minimum temperature, then these plants will be fine and they will most likely survive the cold successfully. But if you do have a cold winter and there are several times that the temperature drops quite a bit below the average temperature, then you are taking a risk and these plants will more than likely not make it through the season. Therefore, if you are a beginner gardener and are still finding your feet, and learning the finer tricks of gardening, I recommend that you only invest your money in seeds, seedlings, or plants that will survive with ease in your hardiness zone.

Is the hardiness zone a consistent indication of weather? No, it is not. Our weather and overall climate are changing. Global warming is a major concern across the world and we cannot deny the impact it has on our ice caps but also our average temperatures. As temperatures change, so will the hardiness zones as they are directly linked to the region's temperature. The map will not have any major fluctuations—yet. But what you may notice if you look at a map of about 10 years ago is that there may have been plants that were not suitable for your region but that you can now plant safely. It may also be that certain plants that used to grow very well in your zone, do not perform so well, or that you suddenly get pests that have not been a problem before. As the poles are melting, insects can migrate further north than they used to because it is not that cold anymore.

While this map is a helpful aid for any gardener, it is not the be-all and end-all. There is vital information that will impact your garden and planting season that is not indicated on this map. I am referring to factors like the microclimate of your region. An example of how this can be different from your surroundings is when you are located in a valley, or near a mountain. The rest of the region may be a bit warmer, but as the mountains cast a shadow over your property much earlier during winter, your property is likely quite a bit colder and as a result, will have a colder minimum temperature than your neighbor who may be situated on a hill.

Weather fluctuations are also becoming more intense and plants are not adapting to these changes. A couple of nights in autumn may be much colder than the average minimum temperature for autumn and this can damage plants. Even though plants may be perfectly fine during much colder temperatures in the heart of winter, they gradually prepare themselves for this cold. If a couple of unexpected cold nights catch the plants off-guard, they will suffer and can even die.

Two more vital aspects to consider are the humidity of your region and the average maximum temperatures. These factors are also absent on the hardiness zone map. If the temperature drops and the humidity is low, the dry cold can be very damaging to plants or if the temperatures are too high, plants will take a punch too. The latter is due to the heat and the fact that the soil heats up so severely, affecting the plant roots.

That is why the hardiness zone map is important, but it is not all you need to know before planting. So, study the map and familiarize yourself with what it means for gardening in your zone, but also join gardening clubs and chat with local nurseries from whose experience you can learn a lot more about your specific region.

THE BEST VEGGIES TO GROW IN YOUR GARDEN

The range of vegetables that you can choose from may be quite vast, but the following vegetables are the more popular choices amongst vegetable gardeners for good reason. Reasons like they are common food sources that most people are familiar with and like to eat. They are also vegetables used in most homes. I have explained before that other than choosing vegetables that will grow in your region, you must also choose vegetables that you like to eat. Say you and your family are not fond of tomatoes, then there will be no point in growing tomatoes in your vegetable garden even if you have the ideal setting for it. This list will help you to gain greater insight into the most popular vegetables and some of their features.

Beans

There is no need to sow beans indoors, you can plant them directly into the soil outside any time after you have had the last frost for the winter. Bean sprouts will greet you with two little heart-shaped leaves. Sometimes you may even find that the hard shell of the bean is still stuck on one of the leaves. It will fall off naturally as the leaves grow and get bigger.

Beans like to attach themselves to nearby structures. The plant's shape will depend on the kind of beans you have planted but usually, the plants are either vine-like and grow up against fences or garden supports but they can also be bushier. Once the stronger leaves grow out, they will have smooth edges and grow in pairs of two opposite of each other. The plant does not make an impressive flower but still creates a combination of white and purple. If your beans have been flowering in abundance, or you cannot see any pods, you can add fertilizer to help the plant get the nutrition it needs. It is only during mid-summer that you will truly be able to identify the pods on the plant and not long after they will be ready to harvest. Beans need moist soil so it is best to water them regularly, from the moment you have planted the beans until you have harvested them.

Cabbage

It is best to keep cabbage seeds indoors after you have planted them. The best time to do this is six to eight weeks before you normally have the last frost of the season. Then, by the time of the last frost, your seedlings should be strong enough to replant outside. The best window to do this is from about a week before the last frost appears to roughly a week after the last frost. This is possible as once the cabbage has reached the stage when you can safely replant it outside, it is quite a hardy plant.

Initially, the seedlings will have small round leaves with serrated edges and they have the familiar dusty green color. As the plant becomes stronger, you will clearly see the ball-like structure. While cabbage cultivated for consumption will not flower, the ornamental types will.

The flower appears in the middle of the cabbage as the entire plant opens up.

Cabbages do not need as much water but about three weeks before you plan to harvest, you would need to water them more regularly. The best time to fertilize cabbages is about three weeks after you have planted them in your raised beds.

Carrots

You can sow carrot seeds directly into the raised beds as early as three to five weeks before the last frost of the season. Carrots are hardy enough to take the cold and by sowing them then you will help to lengthen your planting season. Be careful not to sow these seeds too close to each other. Many gardeners have made the mistake of simply spreading the seeds into the soil and then they end up with seedlings that sprout too close to each other and you will have to take some of them out to leave enough room in the soil for proper growth.

When the carrot seeds sprout, they may look like grass or even weeds in your garden, but do not rip them out. Give the seedling a little more time and you will see the feather-like leaves follow soon. You cannot mistake a carrot for anything else due to its prominent shape and color. Carrots flower only during their second year of growth when you will notice almost umbrella-like flowers forming a canopy. The best time to fertilize carrots is during the fall to prepare the plants for the next spring. The plant needs minimal water and you only need to do so when it is extremely dry.

Tomatoes

You can sow these seeds indoors anytime between six to eight weeks before the last frost of the season as this will allow for sufficient growth so that you can replant these seedlings in your raised beds when they are ready. Tomato seedlings are easy to identify very early on; their leaves already have lobes with serrated edges. Tomatoes grow into bushy plants with leaves in a range of sizes. The plant's flowers are small and either light yellow or white. It is during flowering time that you want to attract pollinators to your garden as the flowers turn into the fruit you will harvest. Tomatoes come in a range of sizes and colors and can vary from blood red to purple and yellow. As there are so many variants, I want to encourage you to plant several types in your garden to see which variant you like best. Fertilize your tomatoes about two weeks before you harvest your first batch and then again about a week after harvesting. While the plant is not that demanding when it comes to watering, you will still need to water it twice weekly to ensure the best possible yield.

Pumpkins

Pumpkins are not only meant for Halloween, they also make an amazing pie, a hardy soup and the seeds are delicious roasted. Pumpkin seeds are quite large and you can plant these indoors first. A good time to do so is about two to four weeks before the last winter frost. About one week after the last frost, your seedlings should be strong enough to replant into the raised garden beds. The first leaves of the pumpkin are round, but have serrated edges, from there onwards you will see round leaves with smooth edges. Pumpkins need space in the garden as they grow long vine trails. As the plant gets more mature, the bottom of the leaves may be quite coarse and can at times even feel a little thorny. It may be wise to use garden gloves when you are working with your pumpkins. Pumpkins make large yellow, almost orange, floppy flowers that need pollinators to ensure every flower develops into a pumpkin. Once the flowers dry up and fall off, it leaves behind a green start to the pumpkin that develops into a brilliant orange vegetable. Pumpkins need watering during dry seasons and you have to give them fertilizer just before they start growing vines that run all over the garden.

Spinach

Like carrots, spinach might initially look like grass sprouting in your garden beds. However, just give a little time before weeding as soon you will see round leaves coming out next. Spinach is a hardy plant and you can easily sow it directly into garden beds as early as four to six weeks before the last frost of the season. Once the plant has grown a little, it is almost impossible to confuse it with any other plant as it quickly looks like a handful of spinach stuck into the soil. Once your spinach has reached about a third of its length, give it some fertilizer to ensure sufficient nutrient uptake for the leaves to grow. If you ever see flowers on your spinach, know that you have missed the harvest. The flowers have a light green color and grow on a thin stalk that develops on an older plant. Remember to water your spinach about once a week to ensure optimal moisture content in the soil.

Radishes

Sow your radishes from one week before the last frost to about one or even two weeks after. Radishes grow fairly quickly and you will soon be able to harvest, so it will be beneficial to sow these at weekly intervals to extend your harvest time. The first leaves you will see are almost shaped like hearts and if you have sowed turnips close by, it might be confusing at first to identify what is showing growth. However, the radishes will soon begin to form clumps of leaves with the same shape as those of a dandelion. While radishes do make a small flower in light pink, the part you are going to harvest is of course underneath the soil. That said, it is not uncommon for radishes to break through the surface, revealing the top part of the bulb. Radishes are probably the smallest vegetable you will harvest from underneath the soil. This is a hardy plant but still needs water once a week and you can add fertilizer to the soil before you start planting for spring. If your family loves to indulge in fresh salads, radishes will be just what you need to top it off. In that case, then you will also be very keen to have success with lettuce.

Lettuce

There are many kinds of lettuce to add to your salads and therefore also to your garden. Some have radiant green leaves with feather-like edges and others have smoother edges and come in tones of dark purple. Here too, I recommend that you play around a little to see which type of lettuce performs the best in your garden beds and is, of course, a favorite during mealtime.

You can sow your lettuce seeds about four to six weeks before the end of the frosting season and replant them into your garden beds as early as one week before the end of the frosting season to about two weeks thereafter. While lettuce may come across as tender, it is quite a hardy plant. As the leaves demand a lot of nutrients from the soil, it is best to add some fertilizer two to three weeks after you have planted them in your raised garden beds. Like with spinach, if you see a flower, you have waited too long to harvest. The lettuce flower is quite unique. It is white and small and grows on a stalk from the center of the lettuce head. This stalk can reach a height of up to two feet. You may even want to leave lettuce in your garden just to see how impressive this flower is. Water your lettuce plants once a week.

Cucumber

Cucumber seeds can go into the soil indoors as long as two to four weeks before the last frost. However, as the cucumber plant is tender, you can only replant them into your raised beds one to two weeks after the last frost. The first leaves you will see will have serrated edges and may be very wrinkled. Like pumpkins, these too have a vine-like structure and will spread quite a bit in your beds. Cucumbers have large leaves providing sufficient shade for the cucumber to grow in. Usually, a cucumber plant produces many cucumbers and by adding fertilizer to the soil, you will help to increase the yield. The best time to fertilize is after it has flowered. The flowers vary between white and pale yellow. Initially, the petals will be stuck together until it opens up later on. Cucumbers need pollinators as the flowers eventually fall off and then small cucumbers appear. The size of the cucumbers you will harvest depends on the type of cucumbers you have planted. Some are only as long as your finger, while others can grow to be about the size of your foot.

Beets

Beet seeds can go straight into the raised beds. Leave enough space for the beets to grow into healthy heads. The sowing season for beets is quite long and can be anytime from about three weeks before the last frost to three weeks after. Here you can also sow them in weekly increments to extend your beet harvest. Beets are quite hardy, but they will need fertilizer when you plant them into the soil. They are also water-wise and you only really need to water them during droughts.

The first leaves you will see are long with pink or purple stems, making it easy to identify the plant. Beets can form several seedlings from one seed and soon you will notice that the plant forms bunches of leaves which all have a long shape and smooth edges. The veins on the beet leaves are dark purple, making them easy to recognize. You do not want the plant to flower as it will mean that some of the nutrients are going into the flower and you want it to stay inside the beets growing underground. Beets only flower when they are in conditions that are too warm. This will happen if you plant them during the wrong season, or too late into the planting season. So, as long as you stick to the proper planting schedule for beets, you should be fine.

Onion

From one bulb to another. Sow your onion seeds directly into your garden beds about four weeks before the last frost. First, you will only see thin leaves that look like grass—again do not weed and just wait—but then the plant will take on the shape of a leek, meaning several long grassy strands all bunched together. All the leaves grow out of the center of the bulb which is why they are so close together. Even though onions grow underneath the soil surface, they too often break through the surface, revealing the top of the bulb. Onions are hardy and only really need water during droughts, but they do need fertilizer. The best times to fertilize are once the bulbs start to swell and again when the leaves of the plant are about a foot tall. Onion flowers always remind me of dandelions as they form white balls of fluff that grow on a long stalk.

Potatoes

When your potatoes are starting to push out those weird-looking roots, you know they are no longer good to eat but keep them aside as this is what you will plant for your next harvest. The best time to plant potatoes is from the last frost to about two weeks after. The initial leaves you will see are round with quite a textured surface. A potato plant is a bushy plant with relatively dark green leaves. Even though the crops are growing underneath the surface of the soil, it does flower. These flowers are small and white with a prominent yellow stigma at the center. When you see these flowers, know that it is time to fertilize the soil. While potatoes can be considered quite a hardy plant, it does need quite a bit of water once the tubers start to grow underneath the soil. Stick to regular watering but not large quantities at a time. After your first hilling, it is time to fertilize once more to enrich the soil with sufficient nutrients for the next hilling. If you take proper care of your plant, you may be able to hill these plants up to three times in one season.

So, now you have a complete guide on how to get some of the most popular and widely enjoyed vegetables in your garden. Which other types of vegetables would you like to experiment with?

HELP SPREAD THE WORD TO OTHERS
WHO WISH TO GROW A RAISED BED
GARDEN WHILE SAVING MONEY
AND TIME

You now know the key strategies you need to set up and plant a raised bed garden and supercharge an existing garden through simple, cost-effective methods.

Simply by leaving your honest opinion of this book on Amazon, you'll encourage other green thumbs to hone a wide range of skills—from garden planning for success to keeping pests at bay.

Thank you for your support. You can help someone discover the peaceful, healthy, happy life that begins when the day their fingers first make contact with the earth.

CONCLUSION

Nature is the best of teachers and if we observe how she operates and base our own efforts on what we can learn from her, we stand a good chance of creating beautiful gardens.

— CAROL KLEIN

It is only human to want to share some of your fondest memories with others. Good memories are special and every time we tell the tales of these memories, we relive the moments. Writing this book brought up so many good memories from my childhood days helping my mother in the garden. In a sense, I wanted to share the beauty of gardening with as many people as possible. I wanted to share how easy it is to get involved in this activity that will do you good on so many levels. But I also got a gift myself, as writing allowed me to relive so many beautiful moments in my mind.

My inspiration for writing this book serves as another life lesson—or at least it was for me. I have realized that it is so easy to make the mistake of believing that everyone knows what you know. I knew that the knowledge I have about military operations, the lingo, and the habits of those who serve in the military are unique features that not everyone knows. Since gardening has been part of my life since very early childhood, seldom have I pondered on the idea that the knowledge I have in this regard is not shared by everyone.

It was only once friends and family, neighbors, and mere acquaintances stopped by and asked me about my garden, how I do certain things, and where I buy my vegetable seeds, that I realized, my belief was wrong all this time. Just because I had exposure to something does not mean that it is common knowledge. My familiarity with gardening, how to start a garden, maintain its health, or what to plant at which times was completely new information to others.

What excited me was to see how inspired people became when I told them how easy it is to grow a perfectly fine vegetable garden delivering a large enough yield to sustain yourself and your family to a certain degree, even in urban areas. I love seeing how excited people get when the advice I have given them paid off and when they send me pictures of crops or even come and show me, with great pride, what they have harvested from their gardens. It is this excitement and pride that I wanted to share with more people and what inspired me to write this book.

I used the most common questions I would get about gardening as my guidance on what to share with you, to make this a read worthy of your time. As an expert in raised garden beds, I had to share why this is my preferred choice and why I recommend this type of gardening so highly. But then, I also took you through every aspect of gardening. We discussed healthy soil and why, as the bloodline of your garden, it is so important to ensure you have quality soil in your beds. The outline of the garden is something many are unsure of and I had to include this too. Some of the tips I have shared, I learned from gardeners who came before me, but there were also lessons I had to learn the hard way. Yes, through failure.

The greatest disadvantage to raised garden beds is the initial set-up costs, but I have also shared far more affordable ways for how you can get started with minimal investment. I am pro-nature and always try to have the most natural approach to gardening. Like soil, plants are very much alive and have certain preferences. We explored how you can use the unique nature of different plants to your benefit through companion planting, and how you can rely on these features to protect other plants from pests without adding lots of chemicals to your soil.

We have even covered mulching, watering, and fencing, three ways to maintain and protect your precious plants. Then we took a quick peek at hardiness zones and what it means, every gardener should know what this map tells them, but also what information is left out of consideration. Then, the final highlight is the preferred vegetable choices and the information you need to have a successful harvest.

Now, you have all you need to get started. You now have a solid foundation to turn the vision you had for your garden at the beginning of this book into reality. Enjoy the fresh air and spread the word that the world can do with a little more excitement over something like gardening and of course, fresh vegetables from your own backyard!

No more excuses, get out and grow!

AUTHOR BIO

Gee Grey has been gardening since he was a child. His mother Beverly was an avid gardener with a green thumb and revealed to Gee the magic of gardening at an early age. Gee had a career in the Military and while traveling the world explored many different cultures and their gardening techniques. When he left the military, he bought a 150-acre farm in the wilds of British Columbia in Canada where he lives today with his wife and son. With his wife, he built a 65 ft x 15ft in-ground greenhouse which supplies them with fresh vegetables nearly all year long. After being inundated with questions about his techniques by local gardeners, he decided to write a book on the knowledge he has gained and to help inspire passion and confidence in others so they may also experience the peaceful and rewarding gardening lifestyle.

ACKNOWLEDGMENTS

Special Thanks to Mary Kathryn Dunston, owner of Dripping Springs Ollas, for gracefully allowing me access to her Olla photo library and updating me on the latest information on Ollas. (dsollas.com)

DRIPPING SPRINGS OLLAS
We get to the ROOT of watering!

In an email from Mary Kathryn she writes:

"A few facts that many do not know about Ollas.

1. Our ollas are cold hardy. They have been left in the ground in southern Canada for years, plus

other cold states in the US. Not all ollas can claim this. There is a little prep work such as having them water free 2 weeks before the first frost.
2. Ollas work in two directions. You know about soil moisture tension to pull the water out. Are you aware that because of the porous material, that saturated soil will release water to go back into the olla, if the olla is partially empty? This works by gravity, and decreases the splitting of tomatoes, melons, etc. up to 80%. I have personally tested this for years, and the percentage is consistent. I think of a near empty olla as an underground cistern.
3. Homemade ollas from clay pots from the big box stores do work, but they do not compare to our ollas. This is because the clay used for clay pots from the big box store uses very fine clay, because the desire is to keep the water IN the pot, since the pot is meant to be a container, not an olla. Our clay is naturally mottled with very small bits of natural debris, which burn up in the wood firing process, creating thousands of little pores, which are ideal for ollas.

I have personally been using the same ollas since our company started, in 2012, so ollas are a good investment. I do clean them out if dirt falls in, or slugs get in…I use a new, sturdy toilet brush, and then flush them out."

BIBLIOGRAPHY

Acres of Adventure Homestead. (2021). *How to build a raised garden bed | Cheap And Easy In 2022*. [Video]. YouTube. https://www.youtube.com/watch?v=pHCJL2Xwl64

Bailey, B. (2016, May 6). *Want to build a rot-resistant raised planter bed that's beautiful as well as sturdy?* Pretty Handy Girl. https://prettyhandygirl.com/how-to-build-rot-resistant-raised-planter-bed/

Benefits of using mycorrhizae in the garden. (2021, March 19). Homestead and Chill. https://homesteadandchill.com/benefits-mycorrhizae-garden/

Best Choice Products. (2018). *Assembly: 3-tier wooden raised vegetable garden bed planter*. [Video]. YouTube. https://www.youtube.com/watch?v=tA7S0jYa8s0&t=31s

Castings - a magic spell for soil health. (n.d.). Organic Control, Inc. https://organiccontrol.com/2021/10/27/castings-a-magic-spell-for-soil-health/

Cat, D. (2020, February 28). *Raised garden beds vs. in-ground beds: pros & cons*. Homestead and Chill. https://homesteadandchill.com/raised-garden-beds-pros-cons/

Competti, J., & Competti, M. (2017). *Companion vegetable and herb planting in raised rows*. Mother Earth News. https://www.motherearthnews.com/organic-gardening/companion-planting-raised-rows-ze0z1802zphe/

Cornell, D. (2021, July 3). *Hog wire fence*. TSP Home Decor. https://theskunkpot.com/hog-wire-fence/2/

Crunchy Ginger. (2022). *10 Tips for planning a square foot garden - for beginners*. [Video]. YouTube. https://www.youtube.com/watch?v=4Tlx59N4rAI

D, S. (n.d.). *10 Main characteristics of a healthy soil*. Soil Management India. https://www.soilmanagementindia.com/soil-fertility/10-main-characteristics-of-a-healthy-soil/3153

BIBLIOGRAPHY

DIY log raised garden bed. (2022, April 20). Adventurous Way. https://www.adventurousway.com/blog/diy-log-raised-garden-bed

Dowding, C. (2021). *Start out no dig, one method with cardboard and compost*. [Video]. YouTube. https://www.youtube.com/watch?v=0LH6-w57Slw

898 Gardening quote stock photos, images & pictures. (n.d.). Dreamstime. https://www.dreamstime.com/photos-images/gardening-quote.html

Epic Gardening. (2022). *The best watering technique you've never heard of*. [Video]. YouTube. https://www.youtube.com/watch?v=AOQayuNOk74

5 Biochar benefits that can save your plants (and the earth). (n.d.). Rosy Soil. https://rosysoil.com/blogs/news/biochar-benefits

Flowers that deter pest insects from your vegetable garden. (2022, February 25). The Grounds Guys. https://www.groundsguys.com/blog/2022/february/flowers-that-deter-pest-insects-from-your-vegeta/

42 Gardening Quotes: Inspirational Words of Wisdom. (n.d.). Wow4U. https://www.wow4u.com/gardeningquotes.html

Gardener Scott. (2021). *Why raised beds are best for gardening (10 benefits)*. [Video]. YouTube. https://www.youtube.com/watch?v=nEI69NU6IHo

Gibson, A. (2017). *20 Reasons why you should mulch your garden*. The Micro Gardener. https://themicrogardener.com/20-reasons-why-you-should-mulch-your-garden/

Goshen Farm and Gardens. (2022). *How to build a raised garden bed - new and improved*. [Video]. YouTube. https://www.youtube.com/watch?v=dPbKcQW3Y6A

Green, K. (2021, January 20). *Companion planting chart - With free printable*. Zone 3 Vegetable Garden. https://www.zone3vegetablegardening.com/post/companion-planting-guide-with-a-free-printable

Growing in the Garden. (2022a). *How to design a raised bed garden in 10 simple steps*. [Video]. YouTube. https://www.youtube.com/watch?v=UZ90rjgIDSI

Growing in the Garden. (2022b). *Organic pest control that really works*.

[Video]. YouTube. https://www.youtube.com/watch?v=E2O_YOqOIZw

Hans, T. (2022, April 15). *Benefits of mulching your lawn and garden - Reasons why you should!* Garden Fine. https://www.gardenfine.com/benefits-of-mulching/

Hassani, N. (2022, February 6). *What are Hardiness Zones?* The Spruce. https://www.thespruce.com/what-are-hardiness-zones-5322799

Home Depot. (2021). How to build a wire fence | The Home Depot with @This Old House. [Video]. YouTube. https://www.youtube.com/watch?v=jJ_5gSThgWE

Homestead and Gardens. (2016). *Building wattle raised beds.* [Video]. YouTube. https://www.youtube.com/watch?v=5c2__yoS2d4

How do worms benefit my garden? (n.d.). Worms4earth. https://www.worms4earth.com/how-do-worms-benefit-my-garden

How to identify the 27 most common vegetable plants. (n.d.). Plantsnap. https://www.plantsnap.com/blog/vegetable-plants/

hugelkultur: the ultimate raised garden beds. (n.d.). Richsoil. https://richsoil.com/hugelkultur/

I Like to Make Stuff. (2021). *Making raised garden beds from composite decking | I Like To Make Stuff.* [Video]. YouTube. https://www.youtube.com/watch?v=ANyr-oP_QuY

Iannotti, M. (2021, October 20). *18 Plants that protect against insect damage.* The Spruce. https://www.thespruce.com/plants-that-repel-insects-4142012

Iannotti, M. (2022, July 29). *What is mulch? How to use 8 types in your garden.* The Spruce. https://www.thespruce.com/what-is-mulch-1402413

Judd, A. (n.d.). *Raised bed garden design tips.* Growing in the Garden. https://growinginthegarden.com/raised-bed-garden-design-tips/

KE, S. (2021). *Concrete pavers for raised garden bed!!!* [Video]. YouTube. https://www.youtube.com/watch?v=i3nY-AM9gGw

Levy, J. (2022, June 14). *Mycorrhizae benefits for plants and entire ecosystems, plus how to make it.* Dr. Axe. https://draxe.com/health/mycorrhizae-benefits/

Lifestyle Reporter. (2020, September 25). *10 surprising health benefits of gardening.* IOL. https://www.iol.co.za/lifestyle/health/10-surprising-health-benefits-of-gardening-128a5e25-09c1-41ac-a526-786fe9672d2e

Little Pallet Farmhouse. (2022). *Easy rustic raised bed tutorial | Fast and low-budget build.* [Video]. YouTube. https://www.youtube.com/watch?v=opRmVrta1bU

Locke, L. (2022, March 15). *Garden quotes: Perfect gardening quotes for 2023.* Routinely Nomadic. https://routinelynomadic.com/garden-quotes-gardening-sayings/

Ly, L. (n.d.). *Marry your flowers and veggies: Companion planting guide to your garden.* Gilmour. https://gilmour.com/companion-planting-chart-guide

Masanobu Fukuoka quotes. (n.d.). Quotefancy. https://quotefancy.com/masanobu-fukuoka-quotes

May. (n.d.). *DIY cinder block raised garden beds.* Homestead Lifestyle. https://homesteadlifestyle.com/diy-cinder-block-raised-garden-beds/

McIntosh, J. (2021, January 11). *7 Flowers that naturally repel insects.* The Spruce. https://www.thespruce.com/flowers-bugs-wont-eat-1316111

Melchione, M. (2020, July 3). *Advantages of drip irrigation.* Plant for Success. https://plantforsuccess.com/advantages-drip-irrigation/

MIgardener. (2023). *5 Ways to help build healthier better soil.* [Video]. YouTube. https://www.youtube.com/watch?v=anTAzOLjtiA

Neodim. (2017, February 19). *The most perfect raised garden beds made out of pallets.* 1001 Pallets. https://www.1001pallets.com/perfect-raised-garden-beds-made-pallets/amp/

New evidence for which vegetables should be planted together. (2023, January 23). Almanac. https://www.almanac.com/companion-planting-guide-vegetables

Nickelson, C. (2017, August 18). *The importance of mulching.* Horticulture Services. https://horticultureservices.com/the-importance-of-mulching/

No-Till Growers. (2021). *Healthy soil simplified.* [Video]. YouTube. https://www.youtube.com/watch?v=0js09p2s0Lc

Noyes, A. (2022, April 24). *What are nitrogen-fixing plants and how they help your garden*. Gardening Chores. https://www.gardeningchores.com/nitrogen-fixing-plants/

Order, T. (2022, November 3). *12 Plants that repel unwanted insects (including mosquitoes)*. Treehugger. https://www.treehugger.com/plants-that-repel-unwanted-insects-4864336

Palsdottir, H. (2017, June 16). *Purslane - A wasty "weed" that is loaded with nutrients*. Healthline. https://www.healthline.com/nutrition/purslane

Paradise Estate and Construction Co. (2018). *Gabion | Raised | Beds | 10 | Design*. [Video]. YouTube. https://www.youtube.com/watch?v=_hvw7m40ido

Plant hardiness zone map for north america. (n.d.). Richters. https://www.richters.com/show.cgi?page=InfoSheets/NA.html

Pleasant, B. (2021a, January 25). *Companion planting with vegetables and flowers*. Mother Earth News. https://www.motherearthnews.com/organic-gardening/companion-planting-zm0z11zhun/

Pleasant, B. (2021b, January 28). *Top plants for companion planting*. Mother Earth News. https://www.motherearthnews.com/organic-gardening/companion-planting-zm0z18amzphe/

Poindexter, J. (n.d.). *19 Ways to improve garden soil and boost the yield year after year*. MorningChores. https://morningchores.com/improve-garden-soil/

Quotes about plant (571 quotes). (n.d.). Quotemaster. https://www.quotemaster.org/Plant

Quotes on soil. (n.d.). Quotesgram. https://quotesgram.com/quotes-on-soil-soil/

Raised beds - Vegetable growing in raised beds. (n.d.). Allotment & Gardens. https://www.allotment-garden.org/gardening-information/raised-beds/

Resprout. (2022). *Vegetable garden planning: 6 Steps start to finish (My 2022 layout)*. [Video]. YouTube. https://www.youtube.com/watch?v=DFLbrwSwgaM

ReturnProject. (2015). *Biochar - In five minutes*. [Video]. YouTube. https://www.youtube.com/watch?v=ehRBw7ffPv0

Richards, H. (2022). *10 Raised bed gardening lessons you need to know*. [Video]. YouTube. https://www.youtube.com/watch?v=VY0nid8qUAo

The Ripe Tomato Farms. (2022). *Mulching your vegetable garden - The definitive guide*. [Video]. YouTube. https://www.youtube.com/watch?v=H1JaHXSssIE

Rob's Bob's Aquaponics & Backyard Farm. (2017). *How to make a self-watering wicking bed / Sub irrigated planter - Stock tank build*. [Video]. YouTube. https://www.youtube.com/watch?v=hL7PgoTlImE

Rohn, J. (n.d.). *Building quotes*. BrainyQuote. https://www.brainyquote.com/topics/building-quotes

Ruth Stout Quotes (n.d.). Picture Quotes. http://www.picturequotes.com/ruth-stout-quotes

Straw-raised bed. (n.d.). Decoist. https://www.decoist.com/raised-garden-bed-ideas/straw-raised-bed/?edg-c=1

Stross, A. (2016, March 22). *Why mulching is important*. Hobby Farms. https://www.hobbyfarms.com/why-mulching-is-important/

Sun Gro Horticulture. (2021). *Raised bed gardening: Pros and cons*. [Video]. YouTube. https://www.youtube.com/watch?v=mntkbT9O1uM

25 Healthy and Fresh Vegetable Quotes and Sayings. (n.d.). Greeting Ideas. https://greetingideas.com/nutritional-vegetable-quotes-sayings/

Vegetable gardening growing Guide. (2021, November 12). Almanac. https://www.almanac.com/vegetable-growing-guide

Waddington, E. (2020, May 29). *40 Nitrogen fixing plants to grow in your garden*. Rural Sprout. https://www.ruralsprout.com/nitrogen-fixing-plants/

Waddington, E. (2022, May 18). *How to make a wattle fence with branches*. Rural Sprout. https://www.ruralsprout.com/wattle-fence/

Waterworth, K. (2021, April 13). *Incompatible garden plants: Learn about plants that don't like each other*. Gardening Know How. https://www.gardeningknowhow.com/edible/vegetables/vgen/incompatible-garden-plants.htm

What are beneficial bacteria for plants. (n.d.). Green Eden Natural Plant and Soil Care. https://greeneden.co/biostimulants-101/beneficial-bacteria-101/

World's best modular metal raised garden beds. (n.d.). Vego Garden. https://vegogarden.com/

Yayasan IDEP Foundation. (n.d.). *Companion planting chart.* Imgur. https://i.imgur.com/3F3D4.png

Yildiz, I. (2022). *Sıradışı Fikir | Damacana ile Damla Sulama Nasıl Yapılır?* [Video]. YouTube. https://www.youtube.com/watch?v=NiqkoPCmge4

IMAGE REFERENCES

Anna Evans (2022, September 18). [*Photo by Anna Evans*] [Image]. Unsplash https://unsplash.com/photos/Z2CVTEdUX7E

Anthony Rae (2022, September 20). [*View the photo by Anthony Rae*] [Image]. Unsplash. https://unsplash.com/photos/ktOsIyRQCM0

Bernd Kelichhaus [Pallet raised bed garden] [[Image]. Dreamstime https://www.dreamstime.com/248332274

Christina Rumpf (2020, September 26). [*Red chili and green vegetable*] [Image]. Unsplash https://unsplash.com/photos/bdZk2REPQRE

Filip Urban (2021, January 27). [*Boy in black and white long-sleeve shirt standing beside gray watering can during daytime*] [Image]. Unsplash https://unsplash.com/photos/ffJ8Qa0VQU0

Elmar Gubisch. [Hügelkultur raised garden bed] [Image].Dreamstime https://www.dreamstime.com/-image213363004

Halelujah. [Wattle raised beds] [Image]. Dreamstime. https://www.dreamstime.com/s-image101067731

Hollyharryoz [Steel raised beds] [Image]. Dreamstime. https://www.dreamstime.com/-image241752509

Igor Osinchuk. (2019, July 17). [*Green zucchinis in round brown wicker basket*] [Image]. Unsplash. https://unsplash.com/photos/7OQ4oekzMzY

James Roberson (13 March 2023) [Barrel irrigation] [Illustration]. Book-No More Excuses get out and grow. Author Gee Grey.

198 | BIBLIOGRAPHY

James Roberson (13 March 2023) [Wicking Bed] [Illustration]. Book- No More Excuses get out and grow. Author Gee Grey.

Jamie Hooper. [Wooden raised beds] [Image]. Dreamstime. https://www.dreamstime.com/-image228388482

Jenelle. (2014, December 17). [*Fire during camping*] [Image]. Unsplash. https://unsplash.com/photos/6C6cEOBeE-E

Kaznacheeva ( ) [Field of Calendula flowers] [Image]. Dreamstime. https://www.dreamstime.com/-image270754444

Magda Ehlers (19 Feb 2020) [Basil bunch] [Image]. Pexels. https://www.pexels.com/search/basil/

Markus Spiske (2018, January 5). [*Person watering plant*] [Image]. Unsplash https://unsplash.com/photos/sFydXGrt5OA

Markus Spiske. (2018, April 10). [*Green-leafed plants on black soil in day time*] [Image]. Unsplash. https://unsplash.com/photos/71uUjIt3cIs

Markus Spiske. (2019, May 7). [*Green herb with wooden fence*] [Image]. Unsplash. https://unsplash.com/photos/2XZ-tIRRt04

Markus Spiske. (2019, May 8). [*Green garden shovel*] [Image]. Unsplash. https://unsplash.com/photos/FwW5fhFKM6k

Monika P. (2018, July 17). [*Gabion frame and stone*] [Image]. Pixabay. https://pixabay.com/photos/gabions-stones-wall-granite-3543089/

Natural Resources Canada (2001) [Canada Hardiness Zone Map] [Image]. http://www.planthardiness.gc.ca/index.pl?m=1

Robert Bottman (2020, February 5). [*Pollinator enjoying anise hyssop blooms. Near Skokomish River Valley, Washington, USA*] [Image]. Unsplash https://unsplash.com/photos/rh8FY8yXMss

Robin St. (2018, October 14). [*Close view of three red tomatoes*] [Image]. Unsplash. https://unsplash.com/photos/4I7836bOoxg

Sharad Bhat. (2019, May 11). *Sustainability* [Image]. Unsplash. https://unsplash.com/photos/TiJPOuJ5n3A

Shelby Deeter (2017, January 20). [*Falling, USA*] [Image]. Unsplash https://unsplash.com/photos/W9BWiLHPiVw

Tyler Nix. (2017, December 6). [*Shallow focus photography of funnel with brown liquid*] [Image]. Unsplash. https://unsplash.com/photos/3nUDkYjoXIY

USDA Agriculture Research Service (2012) [USA Plant Hardiness Map] [Image].https://pdi.scinet.usda.gov/phzm/md/All_states_halfzones_poster_300dpi.jpg

Vaivirga [*Close view of plant in brick raised bed*] [*Image*]. Dreamstime https://www.dreamstime.com/-image197654582

Viktor Frogacs (2018, March 29). [*Macro photography of green aphid*] [Image]. Unsplash. https://unsplash.com/photos/FbuLIGVk1yc

Manufactured by Amazon.ca
Bolton, ON